Special Needs: There May be Students with Delay but None that are Stagnant in Growth

Original Book: I Stepped on an Ant's Foot

By: Hyang-Ja Kim

BAEKSAN

Kim, Hyang Ja

- Born in Goheung, Jeollanam-do, Republic of Korea (March 29, 1940)

- Graduated from Gwangju College of Education, Chosun University, and Chonnam National University Graduate School of Education

- Retired after 40 years of service as a teacher at elementary schools, middle schools, and special schools (Gwangju Seongmyeong School, etc.)

- Received the New Knowledge Award in the education sector

- Gwangju Metropolitan City Special Education Steering Committee Member, Special Education Scholarship Data Compilation Committee Member

- Wrote guidebooks and textbooks for special school teachers

- Published essay collection "I Stepped on an Ant's Foot" and "I Have Written Poetry Too"

- Korean Literature Award, Gwangju Culture and Arts Achievement Award

- President of Gwangju Women's Essay Literature Association

- Passed away at the age of 77 (May 25, 2016)

Preface

In the year I turned 15, my mother began reading excerpts from a book written by my late grandmother. My grandmother, once a special education teacher in her 50s, had written the book to preserve the stories of her experiences guiding students with developmental delays. Encouraged by those around her, she eventually published the book.

The first story my mother shared with me was titled "Sowing Flower Seeds." It depicted my grandmother and her students cultivating flowers by planting seeds and diligently watering them every day. Despite rain, the students eagerly awaited the day the flowers would bloom. The story highlighted the ridicule they faced from non-disabled individuals, but my grandmother emphasized the priority of those who faithfully kept promises.

The second story revolved around a 20-year-old student learning to write his name for the first time. My grandmother assisted him in identifying and writing the characters for "ramyun" while cooking his favorite dish. She also taught him the names of ingredients like eggs, onions, and carrots while making fried rice. Over the course of two years, the student, touched by these experiences, wrote his name in characters on the school principal's office wall, akin to graffiti but filled with personal achievement. My grandmother captured this emotional moment in a poem.

Inspired by these narratives, I began reading my grandmother's book myself. Delving into the life and philosophy of a woman who dedicated her life to special education, I felt a deep connection. I, too, wanted to understand and experience the world of individuals with developmental delays from my grandmother's perspective. Consequently, I started volunteering at a non-profit center that empowers adults with developmental disabilities and became a teacher assistant for the special needs class in school.

As a side note, my father shared an anecdote from his college days when he accompanied my grandmother on a field trip with 12 students. The students, each unique and challenging, sometimes wandered off, highlighting the difficulties of outdoor education. Despite the challenges, my grandmother's determination to provide new experiences and social development opportunities left a lasting impression.

Now, at the age of 16, I cannot fully comprehend or imagine living a life like my grandmother's. However, I recognize the boundless and unconditional love embedded in each of her stories. The book has become a bible for special education teachers in Korea and I felt compelled to share it with many others, even those that are not special education teachers.

My grandmother often said, "There may be students with developmental delays, but never students that are stagnant in growth." Her tireless efforts to understand and guide students with developmental delays through repeated instruction and understanding left an indelible mark on their growth. At 16, I may not fully grasp or convey my grandmother's profound life philosophy, but I translated this book with the belief that her love and wisdom, like the water nurturing the students' hearts and flowers, will flow warmly into the hearts of readers.

Finally, I express my gratitude to my parents, who always encouraged me, saying I resemble my grandmother and have inherited her innate goodness. Their support enables me to share my grandmother's sentiments with those around me.

Contents

1. My Mother is Ill

I woke up to the sound of the telephone ringing. I hurriedly picked up the call, thinking it might be from my eldest daughter who lives in America. She often called around this time because she was not accustomed to the time difference. However, as I asked who the caller was, I was met with a heavy silence – most likely not my daughter. Even though it was probably a prank call, I insisted on gently asking for the caller's identity, "Who is it?"

After a long pause, I heard the voice of the boy, about the age of fourteen or fifteen. Swallowing back tears, he whimpered, "My mother is ill."

"Alright, who is this?" I urged gently, "Take your time and tell me more about it without crying."

Suddenly, with the sound of someone grasping the phone out of his hand, the call ended. There was no chance I could go back to

sleep after what had just happened. The clock on the wall pointed to 3:30 a.m.. Just then, a thought flashed across my mind. Putting together the slow speech, constant stuttering, and lisp, I was certain that the boy over the phone was Young-woong. I immediately took out my personal phonebook and searched for his landline number.

However, I was not able to dial the numbers right away. If my assumption proved wrong, calling a student's parents at this hour would only be an act of sheer recklessness.

Nevertheless, the voice crying out the words, "My mother is ill" seemed too desperate to ignore. After a moment of hesitation, I gathered up my courage and turned the dial. Someone picked up the phone, but nobody spoke. Blood rushed to my face. I was about to put the telephone down, convincing myself that it was better not to receive an answer, when a croaking voice finally answered.

"Who is it?"

"Is this Young-woong's mother?"

"That child is so immature... calling his teacher this late. There aren't any problems..."

"Hello, I heard something in the previous call with

your son. Are you perhaps ill?"

I pressed for an answer. However, the only thing heard from her were groans until the call ended. There was no point in waiting anymore. I decided to go to the child's house. My husband was fast asleep, so instead of waking him, I wrote him a note and headed out of the house alone. Fortunately, the illness was simply food poisoning. Thanks to her son, the mother was fully cured after four days.

As the saying goes in Korea, "the ugly curved trees protect the grave."

Young-woong, the youngest child who was always ill-treated because of his inadequate behavior and lack of intelligence compared to his two siblings, had protected his mother.

"The curved trees do indeed protect the grave, don't they?"

This was what Young-woong's mother said after her recovery. With tears at the brim of her eyes, she expressed how proud she was of her son's actions.

Usually, Young-woong was the child that could not make eye contact. He was always looking down and stuttering every time he spoke. No one could have ever guessed what he was thinking. However, when confronted with an unexpected and potentially dangerous situation, he autonomously decided and come to the conclusion that he should ask for help.

There was no greater gift he could have given me other than to call me at that moment to seek my help. I could not have been more thankful.

I learned an important lesson from Young-woong as a special education teacher: although children with developmental disorders may be more delayed in learning than others in their cohort, none of them are permanently stagnant in growth.

2. I Hate My Teacher

Today, my third-grade female students joined the general education cooking class. The objective was to have the students learn how to cook fried rice. The cooking lessons started in the first period and continued throughout the school day. My students were assigned to the 4th period class, which means they would be able to eat their handmade fried rice for lunch, making us feel lucky. Students eagerly watched the clock, impatiently waiting for their turn to cook. The delicious aroma of stir-frying from the cooking class filled the other classrooms, disrupting all the other academic classes throughout the day.

Yesterday, I prepared aprons, chef hats, and sanitary masks for my students to use in the cooking class. I even took the children to the salon for hair washing and trimming, aligning with the current trend.

As the beaming students entered the cooking class-room with their new fresh, clean appearance, I empha-sized once more, "Hey kids, you need to listen to the teacher, carefully. Okay? When you guys are cutting the carrots and potatoes, you need to be careful not to cut your fingers. When you are cooking rice in the pan, you need to be careful not to get burnt." It was as if I had left them alone on a waterside. The students, in a loud and clear voice, replied, " Yes, Ms. Kim, we promise. We will cook the rice well and give some to you and the younger students."

All of these students had either genetic or acquired mental disorders, yet they were placed in a regular public school because they possessed the skills to comprehend and learn. Ethically, those disabled students should be able to have equal educational opportunities, not segre-gation, to ensure a chance for them to live lives similar to children without disabilities. However, aspects of educa-tion that demand specialized teaching or communication are handled by teachers with degrees in special education.

The bell rang, signaling the end of the 4th period. I hastened toward the cooking room, my mind filled with both curiosity and worry. Unlike how I expected, as soon as I turned the corner of the hallway to the cooking room, my six students were sitting there, crouched on the floor. When they noticed my presence, the students ran toward me, immediately bursting into tears.

"Why are you crying like a little kid? Did you enjoy the lesson? Why are you guys sitting outside instead of eating the fried rice you made?"

I asked them almost in a demanding manner, but all that could be heard were the sounds of sniffling and sobbing. Then, one student cried out, "The teacher told us to play outside. I hate that teacher", but could not complete the explanation.

A surge of rage swept through me. I rushed to the cooking room, wanting to confront the teacher immediately, so the lesson was still in progress. I wanted to confront the teacher right at that moment, but I decided to wait until the end of the lesson. However, the more I thought about the situation while waiting, the more I realized that this was not an issue for me to rage at the teacher. The cooking teacher was new, likely my daughter's age, and probably had no experience with children who have developmental delays. How much did I know when I was her age?

When the class neared its end, I entered the classroom with my students. I was concerned that the teacher would be too apologetic and I felt guilty that I had not informed her about my students in advance. When the young and beautiful teacher noticed me standing by the door, she instantly blurted out, "Ms. Kim, how can you send kids like them to my class? If there is an accident, who would be responsible for it? I've left some fried rice over there. Take it for those kids."

It was as if lightning had struck. Whether she was right or wrong was not the issue. I was shocked by her audacity to speak so bluntly to an elder, showing how the new generation perceived such behavior as normal. I calmed myself down constantly as I gathered my thoughts.

The cooking teacher was popular among many students, especially due to our predominantly middle-aged staff. Teens admired her for her height and beauty. My students often praised her, comparing her to an actress, and they always enjoyed participating in her classes. But today, they refused the fried rice that she offered. Even after my urging, they pushed me back to our classroom.

I sat across from the cooking teacher with a cup of tea in my hand. I tried to talk not as a colleague or elder but from a parent's standpoint. I suggested exploring better methods of guiding students together.

These students with acquired mental disorders deserve respect for their rights and humanity. They should be treated equally. Eventually, these children need the ability to be independent and get along with others. I believe that they need the opportunity to observe and learn from the daily lives of non-disabled students. I shared an experience of a student with an acquired mental disorder, understanding and assisting others, allowing them to foster great character.

Additionally, I gave practical advice based on my previous experiences, suggested that in similar situations, assigning one of the disabled students to each group, with a manageable role or, paring them a helper could provide better opportunities to interact and learn from other students.

It has already been three years since I volunteered to

teach students with genetic or acquired mental disorders. Having spent 20 years of my career teaching non-disabled students, I felt compelled to dedicate the rest of my career to teaching students who are often excluded from conventional learning. I began this journey believing that teaching intelligent students was commonplace, but teaching disabled students is something one cannot do without extraordinary patience and, a deep commitment to volunteering. I was confident that one's sincerity and support toward students would suffice. However, today's experience shattered my misconceptions, revealing my though process as arrogant and flawed.

Today, in many developed countries, including South Korea, special education is integrated into institutions as inclusive education. This reflects moral principles advocating equal rights and opportunities for all in society. On top of that, collaboration between disabled and non-disabled students fosters greater understanding of disabled students, and the desirable actions of non-disabled students could inspire the disabled students.

However, special education encounters resistance in general school communities due to prevalent misconceptions. Many perceive special and regular education as entirely separate. All educators must know the importance of special education before entering classrooms. Knowledge without action is useless. Effective special education requires cooperation from all educators.

Until my commitment to my students fades, I will engage in calm discussions with those who disregard the rights of disabled students. I will strive to convey that despite developmental disabilities, these children possess the same creativity and potential as their non-disabled students.

Nothing will be more rewarding than witnessing these children flourish and become confident members of the society.

3. First Day of School Sketch

Today is the first day of school for new students, a day that is full of excitement for the first encounter. The heat of high expectations and hopes of children warmed up the school. The chilly breeze of winter is slowly fading away.

Every year, some people feel extra colder than everyone else on this day. People whose hearts and bodies are both afflicted by an overwhelming cold: children with developmental delays and their parents.

Children with developmental delays have their ways of surviving. When that ability is brought up to the surface, these children can gain social independence. However, parents of those children always tend to conclude that there's nothing that can be done. Because these parents are consumed with guilt for their children's disability, thinking that it is their fault, their mindset is exhausted to its limits due to the burden of their children's disability.

I gathered all parents and students into a heart-warming classroom, aiming to create a welcoming environment. I offered them each a new pair of slippers and organized their shoes neatly. As soon as they entered the classroom, decorated with students' names on colorful balloons, mini firecrackers went off, along with the celebrating song sung by eighth and ninth students.

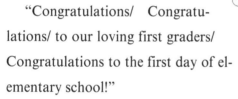

"Congratulations/ Congratulations/ to our loving first graders/ Congratulations to the first day of elementary school!"

After the song ended, the classroom was filled with cheers and applause. The beginning of the "seventh graders' welcoming event" was completed successfully. Yeong-chul, a ninth grader this year, had taken the director and production role. Although he had a visual impairment, he did his best to use the skills he earned from the celebrations over the last two years. I complimented him in front of many people, saying that Yeong-chul would become a great event business planner in the future.

The second portion of the event was taken on by me. I

had everyone sitting in a circle, around an electric heater and offered a warm cup of tea to everyone.

I waited until the parents and the students were relaxed enough to introduce themselves comfortably. When everybody finished saying their names and applauding, the parents one by one stood up from the circle and held the children's hand to look around the classroom. I used the school-year vacation time to paint the walls in a brighter color and decorated the window side with a gorgeous floral curtain along with a pot of yellow freesia flowers. Inside the large fish bowl with an air pump, a family of gold fish danced as part of celebratory gathering.

On one side of the wall, there was a large mirror. I intended for students to observe their own expressions while practicing communication skills and notice how they appear to others. Then, they can judge themselves and learn to talk more naturally.

Apart from everything, the best thing about our classroom is that it is filled with the most advanced, 21st-century technology. Along with 586 Pentium and a 37-inch large color monitor, visual presenter, and color printer, there was also an advanced teacher's desk, karaoke, and

20 sets of computers for each student and teacher. Because it is difficult to install these advanced technologies currently, this meant that there was a lot of consideration toward the disabled and special education.

There was a sense of relief in all of the parents' faces and their eyes started to shine with life. The parents of Lena Maria, a wonderful gospel singer who was born with no arms and a short left leg that wrote "My Life", were told to hand over their daughter to the orphanage, but they said, "Although the child doesn't have two arms and a leg, she needs a family."

"The parent needs to change for the child to change and if the child changes, the society changes. A change in society leads to a change in its country."

This is what I learned from teaching as a special educator.

4. A Compliment Makes a Miracle

As I was about to leave work, a graduate, Kyung-joon, and his mother unexpectedly visited me. After graduating high school, he was hired at a farm that raises dairy cattle. He wanted to tell me this good news in person.

My heart felt overwhelmed; I couldn't process the information thrown at me when the grown-up boy embraced me warmly.

Kyung-joon's mother, standing beside him, started to express her gratitude in the Gwangju dialect.

"Ms. Kim, thank you very much. Forget all the past grievances. Kyung-joon finally got to his senses and got a job, I thought you should be the first one to know."

It felt as if all the hardship he had caused me over the three years had been completely washed away completely. He seemed to have grown his mustache, making him look more like an adult, but his awkwardness as he stood in front of me was the same as in the old days.

Kyung-joon first joined the special education program when he was 16 years old. He was healthier and more active than children of his age, but due to an unknown delay in his development, he acquired a mental disorder.

At the beginning of his first year at the school, there was an accident where he was lost on the way home from school. However, thanks to the help of the neighbors, we were able to find him immediately.

Kyung-joon's house to our school was a 1-hour bus ride because he lived on the outskirts. Because our school was an average public school, there were no school buses provided, and additionally, Kyung-joon's parents did not own a car. Therefore, Kyung-joon had to take a city bus that only comes around his house once in an hour. This was a very inconvenient transportation system because he also had to walk twenty minutes from his home to get to the bus station.

I always had concerns about his safe journey home. It would have been nice if there was someone in his family that could have followed him on the way, but his family could not afford to do so. His mom had to go to work early in the morning, to earn money to keep on her family's living, and his older sisters were all living apart from their house. He did have one older sister and a younger brother, but they also had developmental disorders, so they could not do anything to help.

In case of emergency, I made him a necklace with his home address, home phone, and school address written on it. I decided that, in the morning, Kyung-joon's mother would walk him to the bus stop. After school, I dropped him off at the bus stop, by the time his mother got off of work. Everyday, I would ask the bus driver to make sure that Kyung-joon gets off the bus at the right stop. I always checked whether he got home safely, with a call from his mother. This routine continued well for a while.

Then, the accident occurred. On that day, I once again asked the bus driver to drop Kyung-joon off at the right stop. However, Kyung-joon had not arrived home until 4 a.m..

Although he might not have been the most clever child that his parents could have had, Kyung-joon was their precious child that could not even be swapped with the world. While I was internally boiling with fear, Kyung-joon's mother constantly demanded in a teary voice, "I kept giving birth to daughters until I got an eldest son of the family in my old age. Please find my son."

Then the next second, she would be saying, "Ms. Kim! Can you even imagine how hungry my child is? My child can't endure hunger either. Hurry and find him so I can feed my child. I trusted you and sent him to school. Whom else can I trust? Hurry and find him."

She was 100 times correct. After quite some time, she said in a strengthless voice, "Well, I have the responsibility; who am I to blame? Making less money would not have killed me, but I still didn't go to see him and now, something like this has happened. What should I do about this situation?"

Instead of just as a teacher, I had to empathize with her pain as a mother myself. We reported Kyung-joon missing to the police and waited with little hope that there would be a response. This moment made me understand the actual meaning of the sentence, "Every minute seems like a thousand."

At 4 a.m., as I was overwhelmed with anxiety and worry, I got a call from the police. Strangely, Kyung-joon was being held in the police station opposite the way of his house.

It seemed that since his mother was not waiting for him at the bus station, he was worried and went looking for his mom. He must have been lost on the way. As soon as I entered the police station, he embraced me the same way that he did today.

From that point, I grew closer to Kyung-joon and his mother. At home, Kyung-joon was assigned to take care of the cow and water the pepper plants. He was complimented a lot by the adults because of how well he took care of them.

Often, I would pet Kyung-joon on the head along with a compliment, saying, "You have a very kind heart, Kyung-joon." He always got more excited and started wiping the front door of the class until it got shiny, although no one asked him to do so. Whenever he did something nice, I would compliment him more each time and embrace him in Kyung-joon. "Kyung-joon, you are the kindest person in the tin world, and to my eyes, you are the best."

We got along very well. Sometimes, he would plop a jujube in his friends' and my mouth, saying that he had an ancestral memorial ceremony.

I used to act surprised and comment, "It's very delicious. You must have bowed to your great-grandfather." Then, he would nod twice. When I asked, "How many times should you bow at an ancestral ceremony?", he would raise two fingers.

Since Kyung-joon showed remarkable skills in planting and farming, he attended to a high school specializing in livestock. He finished three years of high school very well and also got a job.

Although Kyung-joon has a mental disorder, he was born with a diligent, hard-working nature, and he loved his family deeply. His fare character helped him become independent and receive encouragement and many compliments from people near him. Seeing a student of mine being able to fit along in the society of non-disabled people, I could have never been happier about having the capability to help those in need.

5. A Small but Precious Story

The day begins for all special education teachers' with greeting of their students. They do this not because there is a rule instructing them to do so, but because they enjoy it. They always greet students – almost like a ritual – regardless of whether the day is hot, cold, or rainy. For teachers who have exclusively worked in general education schools before transferring to special education schools, this daily ritual may seem overwhelming at first. However, after about three months, they become used to it.

Therefore, special educators fall into the category of family, rather than a teacher. Upon arrival at work, special educators change into more comfortable clothing and head directly to the bus station, where most students are dropped off. The teachers wait until one bus falls in sight along with another. As if promised, they welcome them with beaming smiles and hand waves.

Then, students on the bus crowd by the window and cheer, "Ms. Kim! Ms. Kim!", much like a couple that has been apart for an extended period.

Each homeroom teacher waits in front of the bus's front door until their students start getting off. They get into the bus and help the students that cannot properly walk on their own and have other students walk.

Special educators embody the living definition of humanism and – perhaps, descendents – of Anne Sullivan. Being a part of them and taking a part in special education is a gift from god.

Today, as I reached work, I changed into casual clothing and headed to the bus station. All of my students got off the bus, but Sung-wook was nowhere to be found. I went into the bus and asked the bus driver, "has Sung-wook been on the bus today?"

Suddenly, an unpleasant scent filled up my nose. Sung-wook was at the back seat of the bus, squatting oddly in a position that gave away what he was doing.

Sung-wook often experiences these accidents around

this time. His mother assists him in going to the bathroom in the morning, but when she wakes up late or goes out, such incidents occur.

From experience, I learned that the location where Sung-wook goes through an accident varies within a 5-minutes window. If the bus arrived five minutes late, he would do his business on the bus like today. If the bus arrives 5 minutes early, he usually has sudden, unplanned bowel activities in the school hallway.

I cleaned the fecal matter with water and sprayed fresheners on the bus. Whenever this happens, I always feel sorry for the bus driver. Sung-wook had gotten his underwear and outerwear dirty, so I brought him to my classroom to clean him up with warm water. Then, I dressed him in the clothes that I had in his locker for emergency situations.

I am able to take care of these situations calmly now, but at first, I wanted to run away and hide.

It was a winter day at the middle school where I previously taught special education. Winter break was approaching, when an unpleasant odor pinched my nose. It seemed that someone in my classroom had an accident, but I was not able to figure out who had done it. Therefore, I put my nose at each student's hips to figure out that Joon-tae was the one who had done it. He was the student that always got to school by his father's car. I grabbed a part of his pants and saw that it was all a mess. By the time I noticed, Joon-tae's father had already left for work. My colleague clogged her nose and ran away.

I asked myself, 'if this child was my younger brother or son, would I have left him to shiver in coldness?'

I repeatedly questioned myself and the answer was "no" each time. I sent all of my students to their integrated classes and quickly started heating up a pot of water on a heater. I took off his clothing and started washing him off. It seemed that he had been in this situation since the morning, before he came to school. His fecal matter had already dried on his skin. I asked a colleague that had a free period, if I could borrow a new pair of socks and underwear. I also picked out the uniforms that were in the best condition from the donation pile. Once everything was taken care of, I sat Joon-tae down by the fireplace.

"It must be cold. From now on, you should go to the bathroom in the morning, as soon as you wake up."

The child had his face down and did not say anything. I opened the class window and sprayed the air freshener in the classroom. I gathered back the other students and made it seem like Joon-tae had also gone to the integrated classroom.

Joon-tae was a student, who made me more humane. He had given me a mature mindset that led me to be able to take care of Sung-wook like today.

Special educators take care of their students every day, helping them eat and change their clothes when they urinate on their pants. In cases of illness of injury, special educators rush to the nurse, carrying their students on their back. When students seem to be lonely or sad, we approach them like a friend or a mother to tell them, "you can do it" and to hold them in a big embrace.

Special education has enriched me with experiences that have enhanced my humanity.

6. A Certain Prayer

We're climbing up a mountain.

"Ms. Kim, hurry up."

Today, my steps are a little slower than usual. If I were hiking alone, I would be more relaxed, resting as I go, listening to the birds chirping, and admiring the flowers. However, today is an extreme workout day for the special education students, so I cannot lag behind.

I walk faster, planning to catch up with the group. Ki-wook, who was waiting for me, starts running up quickly. I can catch a glimpse of him running as fast as a rabbit through the pine trees. I cry out, "Let's go together, you'll be in trouble if you go alone", but I am not even close to catching up.

A feeling of fear rushes through my body. Ki-wook is a student that has autism spectrum disorder and often does things that are unexpected, always causing heartaches to those nearby.

Suddenly, my back is drenched in cold sweat, and my heart hammers inside of my chest as I recall an incident from early March. On that fateful day, he ran away alone while we were together.

I tried to get help from the other hikers around, but because Ki-wook was so strong and fast, nobody could hold on to him. In a matter of seconds, he disappeared. I described Ki-wook's appearance to all the hikers coming down and tried to find any witnesses. One person claimed that they had seen Ki-wook, but the happiness did not last long. Apparently, he was running downhill towards the newly constructed neighborhood while screaming.

I gained help from nearby hikers. When I explained the situation to them, they must have realized that I could not manage to bring Ki-wook by myself. We split into groups and followed every path that leads to the neighborhood. We also went down towards the big road, but it was no good. On the 8th lane, there were a lot of cars racing at a high speed.

Many bad outcomes and imaginations filled my head, causing my legs to shake and my breathing becoming uncontrollable. If I had a high blood pressure, I would have fainted right then. The cars of the darkening street looked like a group of grim reapers.

"Dear God, please protect this little child. Please let him be able to go home."

With heavy steps, I slowly walked down the mountain. I had trusted my over 10 years of special education teaching experience, and I had nothing to blame but my hubris for believing I could guide the group of autistic students in the behavioral class without trouble...

Once I calmed down, I aimed to find Ki-wook. My plan was to inform his parents and school that he was missing, and seek help from the police and radio broadcast.

Upon reaching the school office, I grabbed the phone handle but could not remember Ki-wook's parent's phone number. I was distraught. I was dragging myself to my classroom to find out when I saw Ki-wook standing in front of me. One minute, mixed emotions of relief and resentment filled me as I embraced him. Then, I started yelling at him for not listening to me and how much I was worried. Nevertheless, Ki-wook was standing in front of me, displaying no facial expressions. He stared at me as if I were overreacting.

"I was looking for you everywhere. Which way did

you come back?"

"I came the other way around"

Ki-wook had a photographic memory. God, who does not discriminate against anyone, had also given him a gift.

I can see Ki-wook through the spaces between the pine trees. It seems that he has already gone to the top of the mountain and is coming down to where I am. He has learned to consider other people more.

The fact that Ki-wook has come back to me, instead of going back alone, means that he has become more thoughtful.

"Son, Please Look in My Eyes as You Speak" is a novel about a father who quit work to successfully teach autistic children. From his experience, he claims that children with autism are "visual prioritizers." He also states that autistic children's tendency to prioritize visible objects does not originate from developmental delays. They rather have much better visualization abilities than non disabled children, to the point that they seem as a genius. The author of the book was amazed when they noticed their child reading text from the age of four but soon realized that it was only the words, not the meaning behind them.

The author states, "Autism spectrum disorder occurs due to the malfunction of the logical senses of the brain, caused by an overdevelopment of the visualization ability. Therefore, the key point in teaching autistic children is to change "visual prioritizers" to "logical prioritizers." Instead of having them learn how to read words first, it is more efficient to teach them how to read minds first. It must be education that is alive and engaging."

I personally agree. The purpose of education for autistic children is to plant minds into their hearts.

"An active education that connects to real life" can only exist with the help of the patience and hard work of family, teachers, and neighbors.

7. Suk and His Crutch

Suk came to school in the morning with a crutch and a cast on his leg because of a fractured bone. Apparently, he kicked the fridge with his foot while fighting with his aunt. He would often pick up his desk and throw it in the classroom. Once, the principal witnessed his action and scolded Suk, but Suk only got angrier and threw another desk. This became top news around the school for a while.

The children, not noticing Suk's bad mood, kept imitating his walk and playing with the crutch whenever they had a chance. At last, they broke the crutch at lunch time.

After class, when I called the hospital about Suk's broken crutch, they told me to bring $20. I took Suk to the hospital, bought him a new crutch, then sent him home.

For some reason, Suk was living apart from his parents. He lived with his sister and his aunt in a small rented house. Suk's aunt gave up on her marriage prospects because she was too busy taking care of her niece and nephew through her small blanket business.

Because Suk has the habit of kicking and throwing furniture whenever he is mad, almost all the furniture in Suk's house is damaged. In caring for her nephew and niece as a single woman, Suk's aunt, with the help of Suk's sister, has reportedly strived to stop Suk from violent misbehavior; however, rather than returning the blessings, Suk has continually thrown tantrums, even kicking his aunt in the process. Although such behavior may have been borne out of immaturity, I could not overlook the severity of the situation.

It seemed that Suk had been feeling down for a while, but it was not long before his violent tendencies returned. He broke the same leg that he had fractured last time, and the doctor insisted that he rests at home until fully recovered.

Every day after school, I went to check up on Suk. On the first day, I packed all the class materials along with some fruits. When Suk noticed me, he seemed surprised.

He was more confused when I started to wash and slice the fruits for him.

After I gave him lectures on the Korean language and math, I returned home after giving homework. The next day and the day after that, I repeated it. I did not scold him for not doing his homework. Instead, I rewarded him with his favorite chips, videotapes, and food.

It was a relief that Suk's house had a backdoor that was not connected to the entrance. When I knocked on the door around 4 p.m., Suk greeted me with a smile.

Suk wished for a computer. With his aunt, the three of us made a promise. He has to create a reflection poster to mark his behaviors everyday. Whenever he threw or kicked an object, he had to mark "X" for the date's box, and on the days he did not, he had to mark "O." This also included his behavior with his friends at school. In order to prevent Suk from writing everything on his own, his friends became his witness at school and his aunt became his witness at home. After three months, if it seemed that Suk had gotten rid of his habit, his aunt promised to buy him a computer.

Suk took off his cast after a month. On his first day back, I prepared cake and snacks to celebrate his recovery.

On graduation day, Suk received an award for leading and being a positive influence on other students. He has also gotten rid of the habit of kicking his friends and throwing his desk at school.

At home, once Suk's habit disappeared, his aunt bought new furniture and even a new rice cooker. For her nephew, who became a gentleman, Suk's aunt bought a computer.

Suk was admitted to a vocational high school and chose his major as gardening. On the first day of school, he promised his aunt that when he graduates and gets a job at a garden, he will help his aunt get married.

I believe in his promise.

8. The Returned Gift Card

Kyung-wook, a new student, is not able to hold up his head properly, due to the after effects of cerebral palsy. His spine and lower body have also weakened, so he has difficulty in walking as well. In addition, his poor blood circulation causes him to feel pins and needles on his arms and legs.

It was not easy to make him sit in a chair like other healthy students. 'Is there a way to help him sit comfortably on the floor while studying?' After thinking for a while, I went to the school storage and picked up the desk in the best condition. I removed the legs of the desk to fit a sitting position and placed a rug on the classroom floor, along with a cushion. This gave him the privilege of spreading out his legs.

Other students seemed to envy Kyung-wook, so I explained Kyung-wook's condition to everyone, asking for their understanding. Students nodded and clapped their palms together. Kyung-wook became fond of coming to school. He neither missed a day of school nor did he get a tardy or an early leave.

Kyung-wook grew up with his grandmother since he was four years old. His parents had a street stall in Seoul, so he had to live in a single-room apartment with an older brother in college, an older sister in high school, and his grandmother.

At the end of March, Kyung-wook's grandmother stopped by the school, expressing her intention to give some snacks to all the students. She handed me a black plastic bag, but as I was still teaching, I could not check its contents and could only express my gratitude.

When recess began, I opened the bag to give out the snacks. In the bag, there was a box of Choco-pie that the students enjoyed, along with a white envelope. The envelope contained a letter from Kyung-wook's mother and a $50 gift card.

Apparently, she could not help but cry when she heard from Kyung-wook's grandmother that I made a desk for Kyung-wook. She also mentioned that the gift card was her way of showing appreciation and that she would be thankful if I accepted it. I called Kyung-wook's grandmother, saying that I appreciate the gift but do not feel comfortable taking it. However, she responded that if she had the chance, she would have given much more than fifty dollars. She is rather embarrassed that she is only able to give such a small gift. I decided to try and find another way to return the gift without hurting anyone's feelings.

Then, late autumn came around and Kyung-wook caught a bad flu. He had contracted the flu before the vaccine day that the school planned. I felt terrible that he got the flu before receiving the flu vaccine. Thankfully, Kyung-wook recovered and returned to school soon after. Although he recuperated from the flu, he did not have any strength in his body and stumbled often. I feared that if Kyung-wook remained in this state, something troubling might happen. I obtained permission from his grandmother and took him to the oriental clinic that my colleague recommended. The doctor suggested that he drink some oriental medicine to restore his energy, so I purchased a box.

A smile appeared in the corner of my lips as I pictured Kyung-wook's healthy face. I was so satisfied and light-hearted that I felt as if I were floating in the air. Kyung-wook became healthier every day. From then on, Kyung-wook came to school with a smile on his face.

9. Sowing Flower Seeds

The spring rain poured throughout last night.

I headed to work earlier than I ever had, curious about how the flower seeds I sowed with my students a week ago had turned out.

We went through the sprinkling rain to see the progress. The sprouts that had been looking down became healthy and confidently raised their leaves toward the sky. Little sounds of awe could be heard from my students. They looked at the sprouts as if they had discovered a valuable treasure.

I allowed my students to plant as many flower seeds as they wanted in the space that they could control. From the day they first planted the seeds, the students never skipped a day to water the spot. Even when the rain was pouring, they went outside with their raincoats to water the plants. The non-disabled students often made fun of them and called them "idiots" for doing so.

Although they might not know the reason behind watering the seeds, they have kept the promise that they made to their teacher about having to water the seeds every day. My students take responsibility for promises and know how to keep them. Their actions do not reflect that they are "idiots" but rather that they are pure and kind-hearted.

Each and every child with mental-development disorders has a talent of their own. If teachers and parents collaborate to identify these potentials and give them practice opportunities, simplifying and dividing the workload according to their abilities, students will be able to demonstrate their value in society.

It is strictly forbidden to act impatiently with these children. It is essential to have patience and allow them to adapt to repeated practices. However, some non-disabled individuals hold negative opinions about these methods. A more significant issue lies in how disabled children are treated at home. Parents and even siblings often underestimate these children's and discourage them from manageable tasks. Being alienated from home further leads to isolation in society.

A few days ago, my student, Eun-ju, secretly took a $10 bill out of her mother's purse. With that money, she went and bought a pack of cigarettes for her father and a pair of socks for her mother.

Eun-ju always wanted to run an errand for her father, but she told me she is not allowed to do many things that her younger sibling is allowed to do. She wanted to receive a compliment for running an errand successfully and follow her mother to the maternal side of the family's house. She also wished to visit the paternal countryside home. Eun-ju sobbed, expressing her sadness of at being denied these opportunities with a stutter.

When you reject a child's desire for recognition, it leads them to attempt to imitate those actions using the wrong method.

Even a small task can be important for children with mental development disorders. I teach them how to grow a seed into a seedling, water the flowers, and pluck out weeds. When the flowers beautifully bloom from the sprouts, my students will once again be in awe.

10. I Stepped on an Ants Foot

When observing children with mental developmental disorders, you might notice that they always wear happy smiles while communicating in their unique ways. People look at them and become sympathetic because there is no way to understand what the children are trying to convey through their body language.

If only I could express their dreams, happiness, beauty, laughter, sadness, and astonishing talents in literary terms.

At last, Ki-wook learned how to express his thoughts in clear words and write them directly onto a piece of paper.

I feel the responsibility to tell you the story of what it took get to today because it will give so much hope to the people living on this planet. It's also because I want to share the happiness that I experienced in the process with as many people as possible.

At the beginning of this school year, I got assigned to teach a classroom full of students with low mental development and autistic tendencies. Not by pressure but purely because I wanted to. The reason for volunteering for the position that all my colleagues tried to avoid was a small wish that I had. Before leaving my teaching career behind, I wanted to do something worthwhile.

Among the students in my class, Ki-wook was especially hard to communicate with. He would stare blankly for a long time but never escaped his bubble. Then, it was a day in mid-May with Acacia flowers blooming endlessly. I was walking up the hill behind school, hand-in-hand with Ki-wook. Stepping into the entrance, the scent of Acacia flowers poked our noses. Ki-wook flared his nostrils and started climbing the hill speedily.

"Do you know what this smell is?"

"The smell of my mom's makeup"

"Yes, that's right! It's the smell of your mother's makeup products."

"My mother's makeup must have followed us on the hike"

"Do you want to go find it?"

We followed the scent of the flowers. On a rather low side of the hill, the Acacia tree habitat appeared. The white petals flowing in the wind like snow. Not by the request of anyone, Ki-wook wholeheartedly sang "Fruit Garden Way." Together, we sang in unison beneath the Acacia trees.

Ki-wook was a boy with a lot of emotions flowed in his heart. The poem that he wrote, inspired by the words we exchanged that day, was "My Mother's Makeup."

What's that scent?

The scent of Acacia flowers.

The scent of my mother's makeup.

Finding out about Ki-wook's literary talent was a blessing. From that day on, we went on a hike every day, dancing with flowers and singing with birds. When we met a squirrel, we sang a song about squirrels.

While resting on a rock, I would tell him a funny folk tale or read him a fairy tale. We would go to the top of the mountain and guess the names of each building in Gwang-Ju, observe how much the World Cup Stadium has been built, and find where Ki-wook's house is. In the midst of that, Ki-wook obtained a sense of direction.

The heartfelt boy would look over the whole of Gwang-Ju City and gasp in amazement on a clear day. On a day when the clouds covered the entire view, the boy blamed the chimneys of China's factories.

The conversations we had inspired him to write more.

"The birds must be in music class. Do you want to sit here and listen for a while? They're singing like 'chirp, chirp'."

"No, they don't. They sing like 'cheep, cheep'."

"Yes, you're right about that. The mother bird sings like 'chirp chirp' while the baby bird sings like 'cheep cheep.'"

"The mother and the baby birds are singing together."

"Yes, yes. It must be their duet time."

This conversation was what led Ki-wook to write his second children's poetry:

Teacher tells me birds sing like "chirp chirp".
I tell her birds sing like "cheep cheep".

"The flowers, birds, trees, and rocks in this mountain are all your friends, Ki-wook. We must be careful to not hurt them."

"I'm sorry, little ant."

"Why do you say that?"

"I stepped on an ant's foot."

"Ants are really small, so you can't just step on its foot. In this case, you say that you stepped on the ant."

"No, I stepped on the ant's foot. Otherwise, it wouldn't be alive."

"Then, how about you write your thoughts on this sheet of paper?"

I'm sorry, little ant,
For stepping on your foot
I'm truly sorry.

I also had Ki-wook practice reading and imitating other poems. Then, pulling on the tangled strings of his own dreams to form lines, unraveling and tying knots to construct stanzas, creating beautiful ribbons representing his life, he wrote nearly 200 poems in his name.

One day, I brought the children's book "Snow White and the Seven Dwarfs" to a hiking and read it to Ki-wook. I asked Ki-wook about his thoughts on the background, people, and colors of the cover page. Although he did not respond right away, he showed interest.

For every hike, we always brought a fairy tale book. I chose the books based Ki-wook's comprehension level, usually a picture book, a short play, or a children's song that is short enough to get Ki-wook focused during the reading.

In the classroom, we also read fairy tales together. I varied my voice, gestures, and reading methods, such as reading out loud, playing a pre-recorded reading, short storytelling, and incorporating the characters from his favorite plays and to create engaging scenes.

At times, I raised the difficulty level by asking more complex questions, such as "Do you think Snow White would be alive or dead?" and "Would you prefer her to be alive?" These questions aimed to boost Ki-wook's confidence and show respect by seeking his opinion leading to visible growth, he showed growth in his creativity.

After finishing a fairy tale book, I encouraged Ki-wook to express his thoughts through activities like drawing a comic book or writing a letter to the main character of the story. Ki-wook especially liked writing letters to the characters of the book. Whenever he wrote a letter, I assumed the characters' roles and responded to him in character. In the end, we read 130 fairy tale books and wrote reflections for 70 of them.

In order to improve Ki-wook's writing skills, I changed the journal homework into an in-class assignment. I instructed him to write a journal entry on the whiteboard as soon as he arrived in class. This approach set a hopeful mood for the day, fostering curiosity about what awaited us. The reason for using the whiteboard is that it was easier for me to correct his punctuation and grammatical errors in real-time. After proofreading, I made him copy the corrected version into his writing.

The topics usually revolved around Ki-wook's favorite foods, and over time, we extended the length of writing.

Following this, Ki-wook's schedule included climbing up and down the mountains behind the school while discussing flowers and birds, resulting in the creation of beautiful poetry. Then, we read a fairytale, and he would write a book reflection or a letter to the characters of the story.

Writing this chapter, my hope is that the prejudice, "Mentally disabled people cannot do anything," will be discarded, that those in higher positions will recognize their worth, and that people will realize a little support from their surroundings will help them bloom their talents in society.

There were people around me who questioned about how these children can read and express their thoughts. I, too, was once among this skeptics.Through reading this, I hope they understand that children with mental development disorders are not much different from us, except that they require just a gentle push to reach where we are.

However, I cannot deny the reality that it is a lengthy process to uncover the happiness, sadness, and laughter buried deep within these children's minds.

11. A Name Written at Age 20

It was only morning when the head teacher was looking for a student that "drew stuff on the walls of the principal's office" in my classroom. Unfortunately, today was the day before the school's pilot research presentation designated by the Ministry of Education and the walls of the principal's office had just been newly painted white. Though the letters written on the wall with crayons were barely legible, they revealed the name of a student from my class, indicating that one of the special education students were responsible.

I went to the "scene of the crime." The overwhelmingly large letters, written in black crayons, made my heart drop.

"Jung-jun Seo"

To my relief, I did not recognize the handwriting at

all and the student, Jung-jun Seo, was illiterate as far as I know.

I came back to the classroom and made all the literate students write the name "Jung-jun Seo" on the whiteboard. Expectedly, none of the handwriting matched the ones on the wall and the conflict with the head teacher died down.

After receiving an apology from the head teacher, I was about to walk out of the classroom when Jung-jun Seo walked towards the whiteboard and wrote his name in the same handwriting that was written on the walls of the principal's office.

I could not believe my eyes! The saying "no matter how lowly intelligent students are, there are none that are stagnant in growth" was proved in this historical moment.

With tears brimming at the edge of my eyes, I approached the whiteboard and wrote the poem, "A Name Written At Age 20," on the spot. Rather than a poem, it was more of a confession of my current thoughts to the head teacher.

The scribbled handwriting,

On the newly painted white walls,

The school, bustling to identify and punish the culprit.

But if it is a name which took 20 years to write,

Would it not be an occasion to celebrate, rather than to scold?

As what is appropriate depends merely on the circumstance.

Suddenly, I remembered the time I was teaching Jung-jun the Korean alphabet. It had been two years since I became his teacher. We started on the alphabet from then on which means that it took two years for him to write the letters of his own name. Starting from his favorite food, I made him write the names of singers, actors, soccer players, and baseball players. I tried to be as patient as possible and created lessons around topics that may spark his interest. However, Jae-Jun mostly slept through my class, loudly snoring. On those days, I would let him sleep and give him my jacket to use as a blanket. On the other days, he would attentively listen to my teaching, making me feel delighted. These days of teaching had led to the miracle that happened today.

The first word Jung-jun memorized was "ramyun,"

which was his ultimate favorite food.

"Your name?"

"Jung-jun Seo."

"What's the name of the object that I'm holding right now?"

"Ramyun."

"Yes, you're correct. As a prize, I will cook you ramyun."

As the water boiled, I would ask "The water is boiling right now, what would I put in now?" Wanting to eat the ramyun as soon as possible, Jung-jun rapidly ripped open the ramyun package. The process of putting in the fried noodles, the soup powder, and the raw egg and waiting for it to cook had led him to memorize the words "ramyun," "steam," and "bubbling." While tasting the ramyun, I taught him the words "spicy," "salty," and "bland."

Similarly, I taught Jung-jun by cooking his favorite food and teaching him a few words in the process. This was repeated multiple times as he remembered one day and forgot another day. Meanwhile, time never took a break from running as we constantly aged. I never gave up hope and repeated the process over and over again.

There were also difficult times. It was another day of teaching them the Korean alphabet. I usually instructed the students by using each of the ingredients of fried rice, letting them feel the texture, teaching them the use, and having them taste it. That day, the students wanted to make fried rice with the ingredients they brought from home. Once I finished cooking, Jung-jun cried out, yelling "My rice became smaller!" although the amount had become larger with all the additional ingredients from the other students. He was rolling around the floor, screaming at the top of his throat.

Nevertheless, Jung-jun had something he was better at than me. He knew a lot about celebrities and the TV industry. I used this character of his in order to have him memorize his own name. By making him write the name of TV artists that have a similar name as his, I thought he would someday learn how to write his own name. However, he always completely forgot everything I had taught him the day after.

Today, he finally wrote his own name. He wanted to show off his skills so much that he even wrote it on a newly painted wall! I want to applaud him for the thought of choosing to write in a place that everyone could see.

Who would even be able to imagine the emotions that had swept through me at that moment? This is one of the many reasons that keep me going as a special education teacher.

12. Strawberry Party

Our school's culinary arts curriculum is designed to integrate with and without disabilities through shared classes. However, once a week, special education teachers supervise an additional cooking class called "Today's Cooking", which is held in a more approachable environment for disabled students. This is to enable students with mental developmental disorders to smoothly transition into mainstream classes.

To compensate for the lack of individual attention in integrated classes, teachers provide personalized instructions on essential cooking skills, such as using knives, handling hot materials, using microwaves and cutting boards, and cleaning up after cooking.

The training typically covers cooking rice, soybean paste soup, noodles, ramyun, etc. Special education teachers repeatedly teach students essential techniques in daily life, such as holding a spoon, to empower them to eat independently without assistance. Additionally, students experience tasting the food during the cooking process in order to understand that each food has a different way of eating. Table manners and methods of treating guests are also part of the instruction. Of course, it's challenging to have everything go according to plan, but I believe that through countless repeated practices, students will at least meet the minimum requirements.

From my experience, there is a palpable difference between students who have prior experience and those who do not. Moreover, when all students participate, the classroom ambiance lights up.

I decided that in "Today's Cooking," students would wash strawberries and present them to guests. They will wash strawberries independently, choose a suitable plate, present them to guests, taste them, and learn about the variety of nutrients in each strawberry.

Although the strawberries were pricey as they were not in season yet, I prepared as much as I could by emptying my own pockets. I wanted to give my students an opportunity to present these strawberries to the integrated class teachers. In doing so, I aimed to let my students gain a sense of pride – "We can do it too!" – and help shatter the prejudice other teachers have held regarding my students.

After explaining to my students, I first taught them how to wash the strawberries. I instructed them that, since strawberries do not have peels, we wash them without taking off the leaves at the top, rinse them with salt water, and then remove the water using a strainer. Then, I demonstrated the process in front of them and instructed each student individually. Once everyone seemed to have understood, the students started to wash their own share of strawberries.

Right then, suddenly, one student started vomiting. I paused the lesson for a moment and quickly took the student to the nurse's room. Thankfully, it was not too much of a big issue, so we got things resolved with a digestive pill.

I came back to the classroom. I questioned my eyes when there were no strawberries left but only green leaves on the table. Alas! It was my mistake. Given that strawberries were not in season (thus, rare) and acknowledging most of their families' financial situations, it was only logical for them to crave the fruit. Obviously, they would have wanted to eat the strawberries themselves instead of presenting them to others. I believe the outcome would have been similar if I had tasked non-disabled students or even adults.

"You guys don't want any more strawberries now, right?"

"No, Ms. Kim, we want more."

I went to the marketplace with my students. Once we were within reachable distance of the pile of strawberries, the students begged, "Wow, the strawberry looks so delicious. We want them, Ms. Kim." I decided to move today's plan of inviting guests to another day.

We came back to the classroom with fresh strawberries.

I announced, "Let's have a strawberry party all to ourselves."

My students started clapping and cheering loudly. Smiling joyfully and strictly following instructions, everyone started washing the strawberries. The happy students displayed their strawberries on plates and prepared for the Strawberry Party.

We sat around a round table, covered in pretty tablecloth, and the students picked out the largest strawberry and gave it to me. Then, they offered strawberries to one another, sharing them equally among each other.

13. Please Hold It Together

On a regular day, Young-suk would have already arrived at school, but he was nowhere to be seen. Concerned, I called his mom, but she didn't respond as her phone was turned off. As I waited for him just in case, I saw Young-suk and his mother drive up into the school parking lot. I greeted Young-suk joyfully, but he did not show much reaction. His expressions were not bright, and he seemed to be anxious so I hugged him tightly. Fortunately, he didn't appear to be cold.

"I missed an important meeting because of you. If you wake up late one more time, don't even think of me driving you to school," Young-suk's mother threatened her son in a frighteningly mad voice before getting back into her car and leaving.

As I held Young-suk's hand and tugged on it to guide him inside, he abruptly pulled away his hand and ran as fast as he could towards the track field while screaming.

I ran after him, fearing he might have traveled beyond the school grounds. Thankfully, he had simply run a lap around the track en route back to the classroom.

As soon as I followed him into the classroom, Young-suk held up a chair and threw it straight at the large mirror. Shattered glass scattered across the entire classroom. I was relieved that there were no students in the classroom at the moment.

Not long afterward, the teachers who heard the shattering noise came to my classroom to see what happened. Young-suk started throwing everything he got in hand– from tables to books– at those teachers. He was making an uncontrollable mess, but nothing could be done to help. A little too late, the principal arrived at the scene and shook his head in dismay – on how so many teachers could not handle a single child. Then, he tried to calm Young-suk down, but it did not work out well. Young-suk threw a video projector at the principal. After a while of making a mess, Young-suk collapsed on the floor and started snoring.

Throughout elementary and middle school, Young-suk always exploded into anger whenever someone tried to get in his way or show frustration at him. As a high school student, this was his first incident.

It seemed that Young-suk's mother had an important meeting this morning. Young-suk, unaware of his mother's situation, had slept in and made her mad. Frustrated about missing the meeting, his mother must have scolded him in the car. Then, the scolding continued in front of a third person, leading Yong-Suk to burst into anger.

These violent actions of children with mental developmental disorders and autism can not only be immediate dangers but also eventually serve as a detriment in their ability to function within society and form amicable relationships with others.

Whether, voluntary or not, special education teachers assigned to these children are responsible for helping prevent such incidents and guiding them toward a joyful life. This is the only way we can rightfully claim the role of a teacher and also benefit ourselves.

Although various methods are employed to address these tendencies in these children, no method works for everyone. The effectiveness depends on the individual goals and the functionality of each child, necessitating diverse approaches.

Recently, I learned about the success of art therapy

in treating dementia and maladaptive behaviors. Patients expressed their anxiety and inner conflicts through art activities, achieving a stable state of mind and improving their focus, ultimately reducing their tendencies toward maladaptive behaviors.

Noticing Young-suk's interest in coloring, I decided to introduce art therapy, to help address his maladaptive behaviors. I hoped that completing a drawing, compared to reacting with anger, would boost his confidence level and positively impact his daily life.

I transformed a corner of the classroom into an art space for Young-suk. Activities included drawing faces, coloring without lifting the crayons off the paper, finger painting, and more. I also play music that complemented the mood of the artwork.

After two months of art therapy, Young-suk's mom contacted me one morning. Apparently, Young-suk was searching intensely around the house with his backpack, for something without revealing what it was.

I intuitively thought it might be the crayons that he took home the previous day, as I observed him putting them in his backpack after school.

Although no one instructed him to do so, he took the

crayons home to draw and stayed up late. His brother moved the crayons in the morning from the bed to the desk and went to the gym without telling him, which led to the morning's incident.

I have heard that children with mental development disorders tend to intensely focus on something, but I did not anticipate it would be to this extent.

Since starting art therapy, more and more days have passed without incidents than with. Today, he is listening to the music flowing from the cassette tape, drawing various flowers, and cutting them up to create a beautiful garden.

Observing Young-suk has convinced me that art activities can significantly contribute to emotional cleansing. I plan to delve deeper into the fundamentals of art therapy and experiment to make a fun, highly participative class.

14. We Want to Go on an Outing Too

It was when I had traveled to the United States.

I was on the bus to go to the train station. The bus driver opened the wheelchair lift and patiently waited for about 12 or 13 minutes. Then, a black man in a wheelchair with a colorful beach parasol, listening to a cassette tape, arrived at the scene with a peaceful demeanor. Passengers started moving busily, as if they had planned it out. The elderly sitting in the priority seats moved to the back of the bus, and the bus driver rapidly folded the empty seats. People sitting on the right side didn't move to another seat but raised their legs. Once there seemed to be enough room, the man in the wheelchair leisurely folded his parasol and found his spot on the bus, taking away the space of about seven to eight seats. Well, it was more due to the considerate actions of other citizens rather than him taking up space.

Looking around to catch the faces of the other passengers, everyone appeared calm. Getting off the bus also took a lot of time, but no one complained or showed any hints of discomfort. Indeed, the United States was the "heaven for disabled people."

This brought back a painful memory of Yun-Soon. It was the day when Yun-Soon, struggling with the aftereffects of cerebral palsy, was attempting to use public transportation for the first time after training with me for a while. When she was about to board the last step of the city bus, I saw her shifting to the right, and my heart sank. Yun-Soon also seemed anxious. Eventually, she got on the bus, and I felt relieved that we successfully completed our first task. I loved seeing her confidence.

However, not long after our moment of joy, the bus driver said, "Ma'am, don't you know that a city bus is public transportation? It's peak time right now for students going back home from school, and you already wasted so much time. You should've taken that girl in your car or a taxi. If she falls, I'm not responsible for that."

Afterward, the bus driver kept making a fuss, but I chose to ignore it. We were on the bus for a while when it suddenly braked, making both Yun-Soon and me fall to the ground. Not a single person on the bus offered to help us. Would they have done the same if they saw their family member fall like that? Disability seemed to be someone else's problem and not anything for them to worry about.

Yun-Soon hates walking, even on flat surfaces. When she encounters a surface slightly lower than the one she was walking on before, she starts to tremble and doesn't move an inch. Walking up and down the stairs was something we couldn't even imagine her doing. Without the help of others, she was unable to move from place to place. Article 21 of Chapter 2 of the Korean Welfare Law for Persons With Disabilities establishes that "the State and local governments shall promote policies to install and operate certain facilities for persons with disabilities to be able to use public spaces and transport safely and conveniently." As such, relevant laws in our country do not lack in scope, even in comparison with the United States.

What made the U.S. a heaven for disabled people was not just policies and laws, but a culmination of the beautiful minds of people who dream of a world of harmony.

For someone like Yun-Soon, she should not have to

be stuck at home, waiting her life away, solely for the installation of a wheelchair lift on public transport. Because her mother goes to work and is unavailable to help most of the time, Yun-Soon must learn how to transport herself from place to place. Is there any way I can give hope to Yun-Soon?

I decided to try out a method. After school, I promised Yun-Soon that I would take her to the nearest bakery, leaving her backpack behind in the classroom. I told her to pick the things she wants to eat, and she selected two chestnut loaves. I let her taste a bit and promised that I would give it all to her if she walks back to school.

Yun-Soon stopped walking and cried after each step, sobbing even louder when a person passed by. One of the strangers thought that she had tripped and tried to help her up.

However, I stopped them from doing so, even though I heard some unpleasant comments. A walk that could have taken 20 minutes took an hour and 50 minutes. I washed her, hugged her, gave her orange juice and bread, and took her home. I proudly told Yun-Soon's mother about how she walked that long distance.

The next day, I took Yun-Soon to a flower shop near the school as level 2. From seeing her water the flowers and smell the scent, I noticed that she liked flowers. It was supposed to be a 10-minute walk to the flower shop, but it took 40 minutes. I told her to pick any flowers she liked, and she chose a small pot of daffodils. I chose Freesia. We were going to head back to our classroom with each of our flower pots in our hands. This time, I promised her that if she makes it to the classroom, I would buy her favorite jjajangmyeon for her. Like yesterday, she crouched down and sobbed after each step. Once we arrived, I fed her, keeping my promise, and sent her home.

Level 3 was walking up and down stairs. We used the equipment used for rehabilitation treatment, stepping with each foot in order from right to left. I raised the efficiency by turning on the Korean folk song, "Ongheya," by Kim Sung-Tae. Then, we took a 10-minute break, eating snacks and resting. Then, we finally began climbing the actual stairs. At first, we started by climbing one, two, or three stairs at a time using the guide bars at the side, slowly increasing the amount.

Next, we worked on climbing the stairs without the guide bars for two months.

Level 4 training was walking one lap around the school field and then hiking up and down the hill. At the steep path at the beginning of the hill, I pulled her up, using both hands. I used the same method to bring her down. I also tried making her walk on her own. Whenever she saw another hiker nearby, she would hold her hands out, crying for help. I made sure they did not help by telling them that she was in training to walk, even though Yun-Soon would utter the worst slurs imaginable. I simply ignored it as best as I could. When we reached the goal point, I gave her a Chocopie as a reward, hugged her, and gave her the best compliments. Once we came back to the school, I washed her hair, changed her clothes, ordered jjajangmyeon for her, and took her home.

Level 5 was taking Yun-Soon to the top of the mountain. We stretched her ankles first before climbing up. At first, she climbed up using all four of her limbs. If I tried to raise her up, she would swear at me and cry. Eventually, near the end of summer break, Yun-Soon was able to walk up to the top of the mountain (although she wobbled a bit).

Rather than a great welfare policy, what makes a country developed is the open-hearted interest that its citizens show toward each other.

15. Disabled Student and Non-disabled Student

Today, disabled students and non-disabled students are going on a hiking lesson together.

The non-disabled students assist the disabled students, some of whom are larger in size, helping them when they fall down. The purpose of this monthly hiking activity is to enhance the stamina of the students and allow both the non-disabled and disabled students to work to collaborate in one environment.

While hiking up to the mountain's target point, unexpected occurrences took place. Three or four students, all of them non-disabled, gave up midway. They all had pale faces, wore highly prescribed glasses, and had cold sweat running down their foreheads. Meanwhile, my students—who have trained their stamina through countless soccer games, swimming, and hiking—were ascending the mountain without any issues.

As I tended to the dehydrated non-disabled students resting on the shaded grass, I noticed a cheat sheet in a student's hand. Then, I realized that, for students who hold admissions into top-ranking institutions such as Seoul National University in the highest regard and dedicate sleepless nights to daily studies without a weekend to spare, today's hike might have seemed like a complete waste of time. However, what do you truly gain in the absence of health? This reality is the result of a memorization-based education system that prioritizes admissions above all else.

I feel sorry that our society frames the failure in college entrance exams as a failure in life, jeopardizing not only the chances for students to grow as individuals but also pushing them to compromise their health.

The disabled students were concerned that their helpers had passed out. They wiped the dripping sweat off the non-disabled students' foreheads and handed them beverages. Despite disabled students potentially having a lower IQ than non-disabled students, I believe they might actually have a higher EQ and a younger physical age.

Today was meaningful, , as I realized that educating students to be healthy is the essence of true education.

16. Gift No. 1

 There is a piece of polymer clay artwork hanging on the wall at the back of our classroom. It was a gift– a wall decoration piece with grapevines in the center of it – I received from Kyung-Ran on Teacher's Day. Well-ripened grapes hung from the vines, and on each of those grape pieces, there were three brown and green leaves attached to them. At the center of the vine is a picture of me and Kyung-Ran, both smiling widely, arm in arm. Anyone could tell that the piece was done by a beginning amateur, but for me, it was better than any present I have received in my lifetime.

That's because the crafter of this artwork is a girl who struggled with meningitis from three years old and is not able to speak properly or even hold her hands still from the after-effects of the illness.

In order to teach her how to move her fingers freely, I decided to make her try sculpting with modeling clay. Once it seemed that she got used to it, I helped her make more unique and diverse crafts with polymer clay.

At first, I had to take sculpting lessons because I had never done it before. Once I started teaching her, Kyung-Ran had a hard time because of her shaking hands and fragile fingers. I looked for ways to help her become interested in sculpting and came across flour dough. I changed the lesson plan to making Sujebi (hand-pulled dough soup made from flour batter), and it was successful. We made the batter, flattening it with a rolling pin, and cut it into pieces using a knife. All of these processes served to strengthen Kyung-Ran's hands and arm muscles. Making Sujebi also allowed her to try the food that she made.

We then returned to clay crafting, using different molds and creating diverse shapes such as lettuce, radish, carrot, pepper, hat, and frog. We refined the shapes using a graver and let them dry in the shade. Then, we painted them with watercolor and used lacquer to do the finishing touches. Once they were fully dried, we attached small magnets to the back of each of them, making them into fridge magnets.

Kyung-Ran opened up an exhibit showcasing her artwork and invited her parents and teachers. As the guests lauded and complimented her, Kyung-Ran gained confidence and enjoyed fulfillment, which, in turn, led her to pursue more challenging projects down the road, such as dolls and trash bins.

Today, Kyung-Ran is working at the workshop where I first learned clay crafting. After about three years of clay crafting, she is now creating unique projects that express her creativity and style. I believe that she will become a famous sculptor, and until that day when her talent finally blooms, I will keep on praying for her.

17. The Day the Talent Was Uncovered

While grading monthly exams, to clear my head, I opened the window facing the school field. Yellow ginkgo leaves were swirling in the air. Although the weather was chilly, female students, dressed in white shorts and red T-shirts, were playfully jump-roping together. The entire field was bubbling with the heat of youth.

SoonYi, a student from my class, sat at the corner of the field, glancing enviously at the active students. After suffering meningitis at the age of three, her left femoral region suffered dysfunction, limiting her ability to walk. It is unfortunate that the child cannot freely run and play.

I also feel disheartened. Despite receiving a diagnosis of moderate obesity in her health check-up results, SoonYi continued to indulge in snacks, causing her weight to increase day by day. Although she needs to exercise more than other students, SoonYi appears to have lost the will to work out or engage in any activities these days.

In eighth grade and going through puberty, she seems to have developed a noticeable sense of inferiority.

As a mother myself, I have pondered deeply to find a way for Soon Yi to enjoy life like everyone else. Unfortunately, I could not find a clever way of doing so, leaving me with a sense of regret. Then one day, I gently approached her with the intention of becoming a companion, at the very least. SoonYi was holding a clump of ginkgo leaves, her heavy tear droplets falling on the ground, one-by-one.

I was surprised at the sudden tears and asked her if she was hurting anywhere. Unexpectedly, she said, "I feel bad for the baby leaves that fell from the mother tree." I was so fascinated that I started playing along with her by saying, "I can hear the baby leaves crying." Then, SoonYi responded, "The mother tree is also crying because she misses her baby leaves."

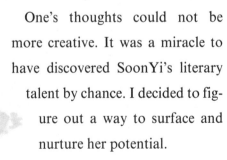

One's thoughts could not be more creative. It was a miracle to have discovered SoonYi's literary talent by chance. I decided to figure out a way to surface and nurture her potential.

The first priority was to help SoonYi overcome her feeling of helplessness by raising her self-esteem. Just in time, the movie, My Left Foot, was screening in the cinema. I had already watched the movie, so I knew its story. It was based on a real person, Christy Brown, who had cerebral palsy like SoonYi and could barely move his left foot. He pursued his dream as a writer and fell in love with a beautiful woman.

I wanted to show SoonYi and her mother the movie in which Daniel Day-Lewis, who won the Academy Award for Best Actor in 1990, delivered an outstanding performance.

The protagonist in the movie was able to overcome societal prejudices and setbacks surrounding disabilities. He was able to achieve dreams and love, solely due to his mother's belief, encouragement, and tearful devotion.

I purchased three movie tickets and invited SoonYi's mother. However, she rejected my offer with the reason that "those kinds of movies only make me hurt more inside."

Having no other choice, I went to the cinema with only SoonYi. Even though she usually visits the restroom frequently, whether due to nervousness or fear of unfamiliar places, she went no less than six times during the screening. Navigating the dimly lit theater with the large SoonYi, while constantly glancing around due to the judging looks from people around, was quite challenging. Eventually, we had to relocate to seats near the exit.

I should have prepared a portable flashlight and switched seats with the people sitting near the exits before the movie had started. I even dreamed of a mature society with designated seats for people with mobility challenges.

However, every challenge we faced felt worthwhile in the end. The discussion after the movie exceeded my expectations. SoonYi showcased not only a profound understanding but also a deep emotional connection to the film even though she missed some parts of it due to her frequent visit to the restroom.

The following day, we decided to capture our shared experiences and thoughts into writing. We meticulously refined and polished our draft, addressing any shortcomings that arose.

When the school's book review contest opened, SoonYi bravely chose to present a movie review instead. To the contest manager, I suggested incorporating movie reviews into the contest. SoonYi ended up winning second place.

Thanks to the thoughtful consideration of the school principal, SoonYi was granted the opportunity to present in front of the entire school through the school's TV broadcast. To avoid potential disdain from other students, I took her to a beauty salon for a haircut, and we had our school uniforms cleaned to look presentable.

As the day arrived for us to sit in front of the TV, I sat next to SoonYi, paying careful attention to not show up on the screen. I gave her some barley tea and boosted her confidence. Perhaps because of that, SoonYi exceeded all expectations. Her movie review, carried by the melody of the background music 'With Love,' touched the hearts of teachers and students throughout the school. The constant applause, encouragement, and astonishment seemed never-ending. The entire school blossomed with SoonYi's story – a tale of perseverance and transformation. Her story even made its way into the "Education Monthly Report," a fruitful result that showed the significant impact she had on others.

Finally, SoonYi had her glamorous transformation. From sitting hunched in the classroom, rarely venturing outside, she now stood tall, walking through the school corridors with determined steps. She even made her way to the principal's office to extend her greetings. Basking in the newfound recognition from teachers and fellow students, she felt like she was becoming a star.

Even in my eyes, the behaviors of SoonYi's peers and teachers noticeably changed. Before starting class, some teachers encouraged everyone, saying, "Even SoonYi, who faces physical challenges, works so hard. You all should strive just as diligently." The physical education teacher, instead of arranging field trips, devised easy games for SoonYi and provided individual coaching. Friends joined the games and played together. Moreover, stimulated by SoonYi's success, other students began expressing their desire to present movie reviews in future contests, creating a passion for literary exploration and critique.

With newfound confidence, SoonYi not only excelled in her writing studies but also demonstrated enthusiasm for other school subjects as well. Riding the wave of this positive change, I continued to visit SoonYi's home during vacations, providing guidance and support. Eventually, SoonYi achieved her dream of entering the high school of her choice.

Even now, she occasionally seeks me out to share her concerns, treating me as her second mother. The following is an excerpt from the movie review that turned Soon Yi into a star:

Yesterday, after class, I was packing my bag, preparing to head home. My teacher smiled at me and said, "SoonYi, deliver this letter to your mom," handing me a white envelope. Intrigued, I glanced at the teacher, and she explained, "It's an invitation for you and your mom to watch a movie with me tomorrow. There are two tickets inside, so make sure you don't lose any."

Filled with joy, I rushed into my house and exclaimed, 'Mom, we're going to watch a movie at school tomorrow. The teacher wants you to come too.' I handed her the letter, from which my mom replied, 'Tell the teacher I'm too busy.'

Filled with apprehension, I thought, 'Maybe I can just go with my teacher.' As I was about to head to my room, the phone rang. Mom answered. From what I heard, it seemed like the teacher was asking my mom to join us at the movie theater.

Mom said she was still busy and couldn't go. With a sigh, she added, 'Watching such movies only hurts my heart.' I think my teacher shared the movie details roughly. Regardless, I couldn't wait for tomorrow to come.

The next day, after the fourth-period class, I accompanied my teacher to the modern theater to watch a movie called My Left Foot. The main character was diagnosed with cerebral palsy from birth, which affected his speech and walking. The only part of his body he could move voluntarily was his left foot. He lived in a basement, writing and drawing with his left foot. Eventually, he wrote his life story and became a famous writer.

When he was young, his family of twelve siblings was very poor as his father could not earn money. Despite the hardships, his mother taught her disabled son to study. Sacrificing meals and saving money to buy him a wheelchair, the main character cried, and I cried too. Touched by his mother's deep love, he listened well and studied hard.

One day, before going to the hospital, his then-pregnant mother tried to move him up from the basement but instead fainted during the process. The son, alone at home, made his way toward the door with great effort, kicking it with his left foot and successfully alerting the neighbors. His mother was eventually admitted to the hospital and gave birth safely. Witnessing his strength, the views of his family and neighbors toward him changed positively.

With a piece of chalk between his toes, he wrote his first word with his left foot: 'Mom.' Though not perfect, it moved everyone's heart. His mother cried tears of joy. Even his father, who used to say teaching him was useless, proudly called him a genius.

Filled with hope, the mother started making a bedroom for him. Though his father initially made fun of it, he eventually helped, but unfortunately, he passed away. Another sad incident occurred when he gave a heartfelt card to his girlfriend, and she returned it due to peer teasing. I remembered a similar incident in my life and cried out loud. Despite the disappointment, he resumed studying hard.

With neighbors' help, he gained courage. They included him in soccer matches, and he enjoyed playing in a wheelchair. Drivers kindly assisted him into cars with his wheelchair. Overcoming difficulties, he continued learning to write. Finally, he typed his life story and shared it with the world. A healthy girl entered his life, and they got married.

I understood why my teacher wanted to show me and my mom this movie. I was diagnosed with cerebral palsy at three, like the main character. My left leg has problems, and my right-hand shakes, affecting my writing. Still, I'm healthier than the movie's main character.

After the movie, my teacher and I discussed the plot and shared our feelings. Although it is uncomfortable for me to exist, I at least still have limbs that can move, and I can speak. 'Let's have confidence! Let's work hard and promise to study,' I thought on the way home. The teacher took me on the bus and bid farewell. Waving, she said in a loud voice, "SoonYi, God gave you the talent to become a writer."

My teacher repeats this encouragement daily. I will start studying hard now and become an amazing author. Finally, my mother, who was always unhappy because of me, will be happy.

18. A Long Trip to Seoul

Today, our classmate Seok-hwan, who loves baseball, wrote an essay that I would like to share with you.

In our class, we have a tradition of dividing into Team A and Team B for a baseball match during our club activity time on Fridays, from the 5th to the 6th period.

Team A, led by Mr. Kim, consists of the following: Young-hwan Mo, Cheol-gyun Kang, Seok-hwan Kim, Yong-min Park, In-sung Lee, Young-woong Oh, Kyung-min Kim, and In-seok Ko. Young-hwan Mo is the captain of the team, with Cheol-gyun Kang as the catcher, and Jun-tae Kim as the substitute. On the other side, Team B, led by Mr. Yang, includes: Young-kwon Kim, Min Kim, myself (Seok-hwan Kim), In-joo Sung, Seok Jung, Kyung-jun Kim, Cheol-wook Kim, and Woong Oh. Young-kwon Kim captains the team, with In-joo

Sung as the catcher, and Jung-jun Seo as the substitute.

The teams are evenly matched, often resulting in ties, but today our team got the victory. We lost three points in the first half of the 6th inning, causing some anxiety, but we rallied to score two points in the second half. The game was ended in a tie at 9:9, and after an extra inning, we secured a 10:9 victory. If Kyung-cheon were to join Team A, our victory would be almost guaranteed, but regardless, baseball remains enjoyable. Despite facing the teacher's scolding for playing in the rain, we continue to have fun playing baseball. The teacher even took pictures of our baseball moments and displayed them in the classroom. Among them, Cheol-wook's form looks the coolest.

- Seok-hwan, a 9th grade student

In our class, even though some students with developmental delays, their physical abilities are outstanding, especially when it comes to baseball. I find myself offering compliments like "You're doing amazing" about a hundred times a day. Snacks are always prepared in abundance, and with the combination of praises and delicious snacks, the students cannot help but revel in joy. Whether it's snowing or raining, they persistently play matches, improving their skills day by day.

Today, everyone, including non-disabled students who usually focus on studying for the high school entrance exam, is excited about baseball. That is because our school has reached the finals of the National Middle School Baseball Championship for the second year in a row for the first time since 1982, showcasing the school's honor and the power of Gwangju student baseball. On the day of the final, 600 ninth grade students from the school decided to go to Seoul to cheer for the away game. For non-disabled students who have been studying day and night for high school entrance exams, more accustomed to a pale face than a robust physical appearance, this is a huge stroke of luck.

In comparison, my students have well-developed physical abilities, and their faces shine with a coppery glow. Looking at them, I think, "You guys are truly happy."

Our class consists of eight and ninth graders, with six students in the ninth grade, and they are the key players leading our class baseball team. Upon hearing that they were going to Seoul to support the away game, they were extremely enthusiastic, to the point of losing sleep. However, there was a hitch the day before departure. The student council decided there was an issue with the supervision and decided to exclude the special education students.

Leaving the eighth-grade class to another special education teacher, I took responsibility for the supervision and received permission. However, this time, parents opposed it. They were worried about what would happen if we got lost. To alleviate their concerns, I promised to take responsibility and accompany the non-disabled students all the way to their homes. So, together with the non-disabled students, we set off on a trip to Seoul to cheer our team on.

The cheering squad divided into 12 buses and promptly departed at 7 a.m., reaching Dongdaemun-gu, Seoul, after a 4 hours and 30 minutes journey. Upon arriving and seeing the crowded stadium with its the open entrance, a concern that had not surfaced before departure suddenly gripped me– how could I protect the children who, despite their initial courage, now seemed utterly defenseless? The worries about protecting these children, who were all over the place like unruly colts, overshadowed the excitement of watching the game. The kids paid no attention to the teacher's inner concerns. Moreover, since it was their first visit to Seoul, they behaved like unbridled foals, jumping around here and there, keeping me on high alert.

I arranged for the non-disabled students to sit side by side with one of the disabled students, but going to the restroom became a challenge. It was hopeless to expect they would willingly go to the restroom for a friend during the thrilling game. Helplessly, the six kids and I had no choice but to act collectively. As a female teacher, I couldn't accompany them to the men's restroom, so I had to wait outside while trying to prevent them from sneaking a chance to run to the snack stalls.

The game ended in victory after multiple extra innings.

Exhausted but joyously singing team chants, we arrived back at the school at 11:40 p.m. Most of the non-disabled students were either picked up by their parents or took taxis to get home.

I asked a taxi driver for help. Fortunately, he willingly agreed, and he safely drove me and the six kids, roaming around Gwangju city, to each of our homes. He was the kindest taxi driver in the world. Although I politely declined profusely, he even reduced the fare for us.

We arrived home a little past 2 a.m. I felt sorry for my family, but who could dare to imagine the feeling of relief and pride that soared like a bird at this moment?

19. The Child Mistaken for a Thief

Cheol-wook, a particular child who has grown on me over the years, recently transferred to a special education class at a different school. I took him to the new school, and we approached his new teacher, leaving him in her hands. I could not bring myself to make my way home, being flooded with a mix of emotions.

Around a month ago, close to midnight, a call echoed from our school's duty teacher, reporting a break-in where the intruder turned out to be a fellow student from my class. Unable to establish contact with the guardian, the teacher urgently summoned me to authenticate my identity. Reports indicated police involvement, casting a heavy shadow on my heart.

In an attempt to steady my trembling heart, I hailed a taxi to the school. In the dimly lit duty room, Cheol-wook, who was crouching on the floor, sought refuge in my arms and uttered, "Teacher." It was a poignant moment. No belongings were missing; Cheol-wook had not ventured into the classroom at midnight for nefarious purposes. Instead, he had left home, taking the last bus to Gwangju after a confrontation with his brother, a high school student. With no place to go, he sought sanctuary in the classroom for a night's reprieve.

Our school, equipped with advanced multimedia systems and theft prevention mechanisms, triggered a police response.

When the emergency bell rang, it was not easy to quickly find Cheol-wook, who had cleverly hidden under the teacher's desk. After confirming Cheol-wook's identity with the police and explaining that he was not attempting to steal anything, I sent the police away. I tried calling Cheol-wook's house, but there was no answer. Unable to do anything else, I brought him to our house. After a quick wash, I changed him into my youngest sibling's clothes, fed him, and put him to sleep. Cheol-wook slept well, but I couldn't find any sleep myself.

The next day, to avoid the attention of other students, I went to school early with Cheol-wook. We still couldn't get in touch with his home.

Cheol-wook had moved to his grandmother's house

in J County just a few days before this incident. His father had worked as a water level manager at a dam, but he passed away due to liver cancer. The shock of his father's death led to his mother being hospitalized for mental illness.

After work, I visited Cheol-wook's grandmother with him. The elderly grandmother, over 80 years old, had difficulty hearing, and she couldn't answer the phone. Moreover, due to her illness, she was unsure whether her grandson had entered or left the house.

The front porch glass doors were all shattered, and when I inquired about the reason, Cheol-wook said it was the mischief of his older brother who attends high school. When his grandmother scolded him for breaking the window, the brother reportedly snapped all the pepper trees she had planted in anger. It seemed that the grandmother could not contain her anger and ended up exhausted. I could also tell Cheol-wook did not want to enter the house for a reason – I could not step away. First, I thought the grandmother needed to regain her strength, so I searched around and found rice and soy sauce to make a simple meal. However, it only amounted to a few spoonfuls.

There was no other way but to ask Cheol-wook's relatives for help. When I was about to visit the village chief for help, my eyes fell upon a phonebook near the grandmother's head. I found a strikingly similar name to Cheol-wook's father's and the number next to it, which turned out to belong to Cheol-wook's uncle who lived in Seoul. Relief washed over me. Unveiling my identity, I conveyed the pressing situation to them.

Cheol-wook's uncle said that he had visited the house a week ago, and the grandmother had not been feeling well ever since. He had planned to bring her to Seoul earlier, but she was reluctant to leave her grandchildren behind. He suggested taking the express bus and assured that if we left now, we could arrive in Gwangju by one in the morning. He then promised to call another relative who lived nearby so that she could tend to the grandmother while I caught the last bus back to Gwangju.

As I was leaving the house after making sure the relative (Cheol-wook's aunt) arrived, I couldn't find Cheol-wook. Anxiously, I searched around the house and between the alleys, but he was nowhere to be found.

The aunt mentioned that Cheol-wook would have gone to the bus stop to catch the last bus back to Gwangju. When I went to the bus stop, I could see Cheol-wook, sitting inside the bus. Happily, I called out, "Cheol-wook!" but he jumped out of the bus and ran away. I chased after him, calling out his name until my throat was sore, but it was in vain.

The rural road, now with rain pouring, was unusually dark, and I was scared. I felt a sudden premonition that he might try to catch the last bus again, so I returned to the bus stop. I explained the situation to the bus driver and asked for assistance. Hiding behind the back seat, I told him to catch the student, Cheol-wook, if he came by.

After about 15 minutes, Cheol-wook, drenched in rain, glanced around. Relieved that the bus was empty, he made his way inside. At that moment, the bus driver closed the door.

I finally had the chance to have a calm conversation with Cheol-wook. He explained that if his older brother found out about him sneaking into the classroom, he would face severe consequences, and he would not receive pocket money and school fees. I also learned that Cheol-wook's father's pension was managed by his older brother.

Only after promising to keep his secret from his uncle and aunt could I safely take Cheol-wook back to his home.

Returning to the bus stop with mixed emotions, I watched the last bus leaving me, and heavy raindrops started falling. I paid a hefty amount of money to opt for a taxi, which also happened to be an unfamiliar "bullet taxi." I requested the driver to slow down, only to feel acceleration. Terrified, I clutched onto the seat. As soon as my apartment came into view, I asked to get off then and there, despite the rain.

After a day of traversing unfamiliar rural paths, soaked in rain, and calling out Cheol-wook's name until my voice grew hoarse, I endured a month of sickness. Although he caused so much personal distress, leaving him at another school for his transfer was no easy task. Tightly hugging Cheol-wook, I vowed to visit again next Sunday before reluctantly parting ways.

20. Finding the Watch

Woong, exiting the classroom in a hurry to make his way to P.E. (physical education), seemed uncomfortably

 warm in his long-sleeve gym uniform. Hastening towards him, I lifted his sleeve to provide relief, only to discover that he was wearing not one, but two watches.

Promptly calling out to other students, I reminded them, "During P.E., make sure you remove your watches and store them in your lockers. Wearing watches can be risky during physical activities." Reluctantly adhering to my advice, Woong removed his watch and left the classroom.

Upon inspecting the watches Woong left behind, I noticed that both were brand-new and from the same maker. I wondered if he had stolen them from a friend or had taken his parents' possessions. However, neither option seemed likely.

As P.E. ended, and the students changed into our regular clothes, I paid close attention to Woong. I noticed he swiftly tucked the watch into the pocket of his uniform pants.

During the last period, I suggested, "I need to go somewhere around Woong's house today. Would you like to come along?" The other students gazed at Woong with envy, but he himself cast his eyes down with an uneasy expression.

After escorting the students home, I called Woong's mother, explaining that Woong and I had somewhere to go together, so we might be a little late. I asked Woong if he was hungry, but he shook his head.

"I'm hungry. I want to eat jajangmyeon, but do you not want to eat?" He did not respond. I ordered two servings of jajangmyeon—one regular serving for me and one double serving for Woong.

"What time is it now? My watch is old and it seems broken. Woong, your watch seems new, so it should be accurate. Can you show me?"

He remained silent, lowering his head.

"You don't want to tell me? It's okay; you don't have to. It's probably around six in the afternoon. Let's go home together since I have something to do near your house."

We shared a taxi. Upon reaching Woong's house, I stated, "Since I have to meet a friend nearby, and I have 20 minutes to spare, I should go and greet your parents."

"Teacher, my parents didn't give me this watch."

"What watch?"

He hesitated before taking out two watches from his pants pocket.

"These are brand new."

Recalling that Woong's brother mentioned his upcoming wedding, I remarked, "It seems like it's a wedding gift for your brother. If it was missing, he would have gone crazy looking for it by now. You should quickly return it and apologize."

"No, this morning, I stole it in front of our school gate."

Only then did I remember seeing a pile of watches in a street vendor on the way to work in the morning.

" Please don't come to our house today, Ms. Kim. I will return the watch tomorrow."

"Well, let's return it together tomorrow, and I'll keep this watch for now."

After I dropped Woong off at home and on my way back home, I pondered how to help fix Woong's stealing habits. The next day, the watch vendor was nowhere to be found. Around three weeks later, during my commute, I noticed a vendor displaying watches in a similar location. Excitedly, I ran up and asked, "Have you ever sold watches here before?" He glanced at me, asking if I had bought something from him.

Unable to confirm or deny, I examined the items on display, trying to find the same type of watch Woong had taken. However, I could not distinguish between them. When I asked the price of a similar one, he said to give only 5,000 won (about 3.85 dollars) with a morning discount. When I inquired when he would be there next time, he said he would move to the city center after students finished school.

Around the time when students finished their classes, I encountered the vendor again. After revealing my identity, I asked if any items had been stolen. He chuckled and said, "Well, I move around here and there, so I don't exactly know where things disappear. Sometimes they get lost, sometimes they get sold."

While I was pondering on how to broach the subject, he asked, "What's bothering you?" I showed him the two watches and finally questioned, "Are these your items?"

After thinking for a moment, he replied, "Oh, these are undoubtedly ours. It's the top item in our store, and I don't remember selling more than ten. There are only seven left because a few got damaged."

Explaining the situation and asking for forgiveness, I handed over the watches.

"Kids like that need to taste hardship... Anyway, if

you're going to teach them, it's better to be strict."

Despite his words, the man looked pleased.

I told Woong that I returned the watches to the watch seller and that "the man already knew that the watch had gone missing and planned to report to police if the watch wasn't returned until today." I taught him that like the Korean saying "a needle thief becomes a cow thief," a person can at first only steal small things but end up stealing bigger things like cows. Bad habits only become worse if repeated over time.

Upon hearing this, Woong confessed to another theft, saying, "Ms. Kim, every time I pass by J University's tennis court on my way to school, I secretly pick up tennis balls that have fallen into the pond and bring them here."

I told him to bring all of the balls the next day. Counting them, there were 20 balls in total, including the ones that had not even dried yet.

When we arrived at the spot where Woong picked up the balls, there was someone saying, "This kid came again. Today, let's teach him a lesson."

I quickly blocked the way and said, "Woong, hurry up and give them the balls." In a whispering voice, he handed me the ball scoop, saying, "I've brought back all the balls I picked up." After apologizing and explaining, I returned the balls to the vendor.

Now, Woong always picks up lost items from the floor, and he is always busy putting them into the lost and found box.

The next day, I suggested that Woong's mother buy him a new wristwatch as a birthday present for himself this year.

21. The Warm-Hearted Children

As a member of the teacher training group, I had the opportunity to visit Mount Paektu.

After successfully completing the eight-night training and returning to work, the principal greeted me, saying, "Ms. Kim, you must be the happiest teacher in the world."

Feeling guilty about being the only one to experience the wonders of Mount Paektu, I apologized to the principal, who replied, "No worries; you'll understand what I mean once you step into your classroom."

From the day I left for the training until the day before my return, there were prayer meetings in our classroom for my safe return. Apparently, In-sung would come forward, lifting both arms and shouting loudly, "Lord, Lord, please protect Ms. Kim from an airplane accident," followed by other children chanting in response.

Unintentionally, tears welled up in my eyes. Despite

the school's effort to stop them, the students constantly held prayer meetings, troubling the staff in the nearby principal room and the teacher lounge. That was why the teachers as a whole were confessing their envy.

Moreover, these children continued their prayers even at home, leading their parents to discover that I had gone on a business trip.

A month before my departure in July 1993, there was a plane crash in Masan-ri, Hwawon-myeon, Haenam-gun, Jeollanam-do, on the back mountain. The accident took 66 lives, and for children who watched the scene on TV, the idea of me taking a flight was a source of great concern.

Entering the classroom, I exclaimed, "Hey, thanks to your prayers, I've returned safely," and they responded, "Fighting!" while surrounding me with warm embraces.

With these warm-hearted children, the world becomes more flavorful, and I fear who might take away this happiness.

22. Oknyeodosa

An emergency news broadcast echoed through the elementary school, announcing the mysterious disappearance of student C.

Although incidents like this were not uncommon in a special education school, the news never failed to send a shiver down the spine.

As teachers, my colleagues and I shared the same apprehension: the teacher responsible for the student's safety grappled with anxiety over whether the student would be found safe. There was also the guilt, "I could have done more to care for the student," and the regret from troubling other colleagues. Only those who have experienced this feeling of frustration and anxiety can truly understand and grasp the depth of such emotion.

Upon hearing the announcement, all available school staff (those on free periods) immediately gathered. The homeroom teacher explained the situation right before the disappearance. We confirmed the missing student's appearance through a photo and then formed teams to search in different directions. If someone found the student first, they were to promptly inform the office, which would then relay the news to other teachers.

Compared to younger teachers, I lacked mobility. However, I had developed effective methods for finding these students over time through my experience.

Whenever such incidents occurred, I would collect information about students' daily lives from the homeroom teacher and parents, analyzing their everyday experiences. For instance, if a student who rarely visited a particular supermarket went there with their mother or family, there was a likelihood they would want to visit again. Such a thought process was common among disabled students. The teacher mentioned that today, during third class period, the class had visited the cemetery on the mountain behind the school to play. Typically, the class went on mountain hikes about three times a week, using a trail on the opposite side of the cemetery to reach a small spring.

I instinctively thought that must be the place. I went straight to the cemetery on the mountain. Lo and behold,

there was student C, peacefully asleep behind the cemetery, oblivious to the world.

The principal declared, "The old veteran still has it!"
And the younger teachers cheered on, shouting, "Oknye-
odosa, fighting!" -- a phrase they used to show reverence
and pay respects to the elder, experienced senior teacher
who found the missing student.

These days, there's no place for old people in the
workplace. Phrases like "Saojung" signifying a retire-
ment age of 45 and "Oryukdo," meaning a thief after the
age of 56, have become popular.

Regardless of the size of the workplace, fostering harmony between the young and the old is crucial. I hope for
a harmonious world where the elderly learn vitality and
new theories from the young, who in return learn wisdom
and experience from the elderly.

23. Educational Field Trip

Tomorrow marks the day when second-year students embark on a three-night, four-day educational field trip to Seorak Mountain. The classrooms and hallways have been buzzing with excitement for the past few days. Even our classroom is filled to the brim with enthusiasm for the field trip because six eight-grade students are part of it.

Having lamented at the injustice of not being able to go on the field trip in elementary school, these special education students, now in middle school, were firmly determined to go. In public schools, special education follows the principle of integrated education, and events like the field trip are conducted together with regular class students. However, out of the total of six classes, all but Teacher J opposed the integrated field trip. The reason was that it would be challenging for them to manage not only general-ed students outside but also children with developmental delays, as the teachers are not specialized in special education. Teacher J offered to chaperon the special education students, stating that with 50 non-disabled students in the class, it would surely be possible to tend to one special-ed child. Even though we all have teaching degrees, it seems that the level of depth and care differs significantly between us.

The grade coordinator cautiously suggested that if my students really want to go, it might be better for me to accompany them. However, due to the mixed-grade nature of the special class I am in charge of, composed of 8th and 9th graders, there were concerns about the disruption of ninth-grade students' class. Fortunately, my ninth-grade students get along well with peers and have adapted well to school life, so it seemed there might be a way.

Other teachers agreed to let my ninth-grade students learn in an integrated setting while I would be away on the field trip, recognizing that there would not be any significant problems. However, before we could celebrate, we faced opposition from our students' parents. Their concern was not about educational benefits but safety concerns and fear of accidents, anxious that their children might get lost.

When I firmly expressed my intention to boost student morale and, more importantly, to change the prejudices of non-disabled people who constantly try to exclude disabled children by underestimating them, the parents finally told me to do as I pleased.

On the day of departure, another absurd incident occurred. This time, it was the parents of non-disabled students who raised their hand in opposition. Although the bus assigned for our students was supposed to carry 39 students from different classes, one student did not show up, even after the departure time. When the homeroom teacher called to inquire about the reason, the parents explained that they did not send their child because they could not allow their child to ride the bus designated for the special education class. The parents proceeded to forfeit the already-paid field trip fee.

This incident prompted me to actively participate in enlightenment education, aiming for a better understanding of special education. Subsequently, I not only worked as a general teacher in a school but also engaged in activities as a special education teacher and parent education lecturer at Gwangju Metropolitan Office of Education and W University Special Education Research Institute. I emphasized the need for active cooperation between general teachers and parents in special education.

I also took the lead in the "Campaign for Disabled and Non-disabled to Get Along Together," introducing activities such as making buddies, camping, hiking with special needs groups, baseball games, interaction between parents of disabled and non-disabled students, literary presentations involving disabled students, and more, to eliminate the black-and-white, oversimplified duality concerning disabled people.

The field trip was enjoyable, serving as an experiential time for coexisting in life. It became a great opportunity to realize that disabled people are just ordinary individuals. During the three nights and four days, non-disabled students warmly held the hands of disabled students. They sang, danced, slept together, and shared joy. When we left, the students who were initially separated by adults had become affectionate friends on the return.

The incident prompted laughter at the absurd prejudices of adults who constantly try to exclude disabled students by claiming that these students lack learning capabilities. During the field trip, even Yong-min, a somewhat awkward disabled student, demonstrated the potential to express his thoughts and feelings through written essays.

"The field trip was delightful. The most enjoyable memory that stays in my mind was the night when we lit a fire and had fireworks. Although I couldn't sing at that time, I felt great because I danced instead. Oh! Going up to the Unification Observatory also made me feel good. When I saw the sea with waves crashing from the observatory, I thought of my mom, and it reminded me of when I went to Jeju Island. Going up to Seorak Mountain also made me feel really good. Although I couldn't see a rock shaped like a cow and couldn't touch the shaking rock, just the fact that I climbed Seorak Mountain made me feel really good. I also enjoyed watching movies in the theater and exploring museums."
- Park Yong-Min, "Educational Field Trip"

24. Eye-Level Education

Special education classes do not follow a rigid time-table like regular classes, with subjects such as Korean, Mathematics, and Science. Therefore, I chose a method of conducting multipurpose lessons underneath condensed daily schedules, focusing on themes like "This is how we spend our day." I chose this approach based on my experience of its effectiveness.

For example, I incorporated comprehensive lessons through the process of cooking, covering activities like character acquisition, counting, Hanja, English, music, and art studies. It could be considered a kind of integrated curriculum. Although it posed challenges initially, after about three months, classes flowed effortlessly. The students actively participated with the expectation of enjoying the delicious dishes they made themselves, and the atmosphere was lively.

The key was planning menus based on the children's

tastes. For instance, we made snacks like pizza, cookies, castella (sponge cake), kimbap (seaweed rice rolls), tteokbokki (spicy rice cakes), red bean bingsu (shaved ice), and ice cream. To understand the exact recipes, I even took evening cooking classes at the S Welfare Center. Even when the children were a bit clumsy or made mistakes, I encouraged them with positive words like, "You're doing great, you'll do even better next time." I never scolded them, not even if they made a mess while they were eating. I respected them, saying things like, "It seems Yeong-kwon really wanted to eat this. Let's make it quickly so he can eat." This approach made the classes vibrant.

What I realized through special class lessons is that being greedy is inappropriate in the context. In other words, having too much content leads to failure. We must be patient, as these students have very slow reactions.

In the course of special education, it seems that my personality changed without me realizing it. People around me said they saw me more generously in all matters. It is true. Rather than objectively judging the dishes my students made, I began to view them as excellent dishes, respecting and valuing them according to their standards. This allowed me to develop an attitude of patience, noticing even the smallest changes, because I looked at things from their perspective. This is what eye-level education truly means.

Today, as I put on a colorful apron with several large pockets, the children quickly head to the sink, aware that it is 'Kimbap Making Time." After washing their hands, the children find their name tags attached to the oval-shaped table. Their eyes sparkle with curiosity and expectation. Kyung-min and Cheol-gyun already know what will happen next. They look at me with eyes wide open. I reveal ingredients hidden in a box one by one. Kyung-min correctly identifies spinach. At this point, he takes out word cards with "spinach," "carrot," "kim" (dried seaweed), "egg," and "rice" written on them from the apron pocket and sticks them on the portable magnetic board.

Kyung-min successfully found "spinach" among the five cards. With applause from his friends, he picks a sticker with the image of a boy laughing heartily from the treasure box and proudly heads to the 'self-praise board.' After placing the sticker under the motto "This is how we spend our day" and writing "Well done" underneath, he returns to his seat, smiling brightly. Classmates applaud, singing "Congratulations, congratulations" to the tune of the song playing on the recorder. When they answer a question incorrectly, they place a sticker with an image of closed lips and the words 'I'll try harder' on the 'I'll try harder' board.

Danmuji (pickled radish) by Eun-gi, cooking oil by Gyeong-jun, egg by Young-kwan, kim by Cheol-gyun, and rice by Min. Today is a truly joyful day. Yong-min, who always kept his mouth tightly closed, found the water, and Jeong-jun found a name card with "vinegar" written on it, just like Kyung-min did before! Everyone receives congratulations after placing a sticker under their name.

Not only do the children love their self-display boards, but the parents also cherish them. These boards, adorned with pictures of the children at their first birthday and their current appearance, also feature attached family photos. Below are photo explanations, names, birth dates, resident registration numbers, height, weight, favorite foods, sports, friends, singers, favorite songs, talents, favorite teachers, future aspirations, awards, art, writing, and other works displayed on the comprehensive bulletin board. It serves to highlight the value of their existence.

The students eagerly entered the process of making Kimbap, donning white aprons and professional chef hats that made their appearances unbelievably adorable today. They formed teams of three, with a leader at the center. The difficult parts were demonstrated by the teacher, while the easy parts were practiced by the students simultaneously.

The teacher started by placing the rice, prepared in advance, into a large bowl. They poured vinegar mixed with water over the hot rice, mixed it evenly, and let it cool. Spinach was blanched in boiling water, rinsed in cold water, squeezed to remove excess water, and seasoned with salt and sesame oil. The students, working in teams, attached the egg strips. They put a little salt in the egg, dissolved it well, spread oil in a square frying pan, poured the egg when it heated up, cooked it until thick, and then cut it into strips. Danmuji and carrots were also cut into the same length as the kim. They laid the seaweed on a bamboo mat, spreading the rice evenly. In the center, they placed the prepared carrots, egg strips, spinach, and danmuji, matching the colors. Ater

rolling it with the bamboo mat, they
cut it neatly into appropriate sizes
and placed it on a plate.

While making kimbap may seem
like a simple task to ordinary people,
today's dish created by the students feels
exceptionally special, given the time and effort invested.
The children shared the kimbaps they made in groups
and relished them, their faces lighting up with laughter.

Children developing at their own pace,

Gather to learn consonants, vowels, each in its place.

They learn to count from one to ten.

Yesterday known, today forgotten,

Always a new beginning,

Approached with pure souls, visions unfold,

Opening up closed hearts, little by little.

Dreams blooming late like snowdrops in the cold.

How beautiful; with trembling hands, and
hearts flung wide,

Unraveling the knot of fate,
stride by stride.

25. Children's Poet Kyung-min

Seaweed's a black blanket
Covering rice with care,
Tucking spinach in,
Nestling imitation crab within,
Concealing pickled radish,
All colorful kimbap siblings

Covered with a black blanket
Together, snugly covered.

- Kyung-min Kim's "Kimbap"

Today, Kyung-min's thoughts bubbled up like a burst of spring water—a result of our shared moments of listening, encouragement, and mutual respect.

During snack time, as he placed a sheet of seaweed on the bamboo mat, adding rice and ingredients such as spinach, pickled radish, and crab sticks, Kyung-min pointed out, "Ms. Kim, the seaweed looks like a blanket."

"That's true, you've come up with a cool idea. Why did you think of that?" I inquired.

"Because it covers the rice."

"Exactly, seaweed is like a blanket for rice. Would the blanket cover you when it's cold or hot?"

"When it's cold."

"Then the right must have been feeling cold."

"Your blanket at home, Kyung-min, what color is it?" I asked.

"Blue."

"And the blanket covering the sleeping rice?"

"Black."

"You can also call it as being dark. Whom do you sleep with at home?"

"My younger brother."

"Who does rice sleep with?"

"Spinach."

"And?"

"Pickled radish."

"And?"

"Imitation crab."

"What color is spinach?"

"Green."

"And pickled radish?"

"Yellow."

"And the crab?"

"Red."

"So, the colors inside the black blanket are?"

"Green, yellow, red, and black."

"Various colors are gathered together. It must be very vibrant and beautiful. Are you friends or brothers with your younger sibling?"

"Brothers."

"So, spinach, pickled radish, imitation crab, and rice... Since they all sleep together under one blanket, it seems like they are brothers, right?"

Kyung-min's children's poem "Kimbap" was the

product of such numerous dialogues which nurtured the sprout of his thoughts.

The children never seem to get tired of the kimbap they eat everyday. If I give them a bite-sized slice of kimbap, they swallow it right away.

"You might upset your stomach. Have some barley tea."

I told them this everyday, but no students so far actually got indigestion, which relieves me.

Kyung-min and I must have undoubtedly been a student and a teacher, respectively, in our past lives as well.

It happened during last summer vacation when the married teacher couples decided to embark on a 3-night, 4-day trip, marking our first joint excursion – an exciting adventure.

The tourist bus was scheduled to depart from Gwang-ju Station at 8 a.m. My husband, who was in charge of the overall arrangements for this gathering, had gone ahead to the departure point. I, on the other hand, planned to arrive about 20 minutes before the departure time and leisurely took a city bus. However, a conflict arose. The city bus stop near Gwangju Station, which had been in place until the day before yesterday, was closed. This forced me to walk a bit further and get off at a different stop.

Feeling rushed due to the tight schedule as I walked, I happened to pass by S Department Store around the time I needed to make a decision. There, on a bench, a boy in our school gym uniform was huddled and sleeping. Pressed for time, I initially thought of passing by, but a sudden realization struck me—it was our student Kyung-min. My heart raced. If the city bus stop near Gwangju Station hadn't been closed, and if I hadn't passed by S Department Store, I might never have encountered him. Was it the benevolence of fate? Perhaps a connection from a past life between a teacher and a student?

Despite the early hour and his disheveled appearance from spending the night away from home, I woke him up. Whether due to grogginess or surprise, he didn't recognize me right away. Kyung-min, who is normally a quiet student at school, kept his mouth shut in response to my inquiries.

The meeting time was approaching quickly, and I realized that I had left the notebook with student contact numbers at home. Even during vacation, negligence was not acceptable for a special education teacher. Clutching Kyung-min's hand, who seemed bewildered, we rushed towards the public phone booth. It occurred to me to call his father, recalling the somewhat unique name amid a dozen other namesakes. Fortunately, we found a matching number after searching through the public phone book, and it turned out to be Kyung-min's home. However, only his younger brother, a fifth-grade elementary student, was present, and he didn't know anything about his brother not coming home last night.

He mentioned that their father had left for work on a construction site in the countryside, and lately, he hadn't been at home. His mother worked at a restaurant, going out early in the morning and returning late at night.

I keenly felt the need for a close bond between special education teachers and parents even during the vacation. Since it was clear that he had stayed away overnight, I couldn't send him alone in a taxi, and it was impossible to ask his naive younger brother to bring him. Therefore, I had no choice but to bring Kyung-min along with me. To alleviate the worries of those who were waiting for him and worried about Kyung-min, I left a message for his mother that he was with me and not to worry.

I hurriedly went to the meeting place. It was already 30 minutes past the departure time.

My husband, seeing that I was not present even after the meeting time, had apparently checked back home. He was worried that I had not arrived even after 45 minutes when it should have only taken 20 minutes to get to the meeting place. Because I was distracted by Kyung-min, I had forgotten to call home. The awkward expression on his face when I appeared late without any contact and with an unfamiliar, stray child tagging along... The trip members, who kindly offered to wait until I took the child home... I was touched by their generosity.

However, everything turned out to be in vain. Although I took Kyung-min in a taxi and brought him home, he refused to enter the house. I barely managed to catch Kyung-min and asked, "Will you stay with me?" He nodded. There was no choice but to take Kyung-min and return to Gwangju Station. It seemed that the better choice was to seek understanding from my husband who looked at me with pitying eyes as I left the trip lingered in my head all day. I called Kyung-min's brother again and went to Uchi Park. Even though he might have not understood, I made sure to tell Kyung-min that the people who love him the most are his mother, father, and brother

We ate jjajangmyeon and ice cream, and while drinking coffee, I occasionally tried calling Kyung-min's house, but there was no news from his mother. I brought him to my house and we had dinner together. It wasn't until 1 a.m. that I finally managed to contact his mother. She woke up the sleeping child and put him in a taxi.

Upon seeing Kyung-min, his mother, while eating a roasted chestnut, said, "That crazy kid, he's back to his old self from elementary school," and then said to me, "Don't worry, he sometimes roams around the streets as if he had been taken over by a ghost. He comes home when he pleases."

After that day, even during the vacation, I visited their home frequently. With his mother's permission, I brought Kyung-min to my house too. I learned that he enjoyed orange juice. I took him to a Chinese restaurant and bought him jjajangmyeon. Without saying a word, he responded to my questions by nodding. According to his mother, he only spoke until the third grade of elementary school, and after that, he stopped answering questions and frequently ran away, causing her to worry a lot. Kyung-min's homeroom teacher suggested that it might be better to send him to a special education class, and the mother agreed. The younger brother seemed to be more robust and smarter than Kyung-min. If strangers were to see them, they would have thought the younger brother was the older one.

Three months later, Kyung-min began to speak. He said his brother was scary, and their parents only favored his brother. I then also talked to the brother - I could guess the reason why Kyung-min lost his voice and ran away. When Kyung-min entered the 4th grade, his father left for a construction site in another city, and his mother worked late at the restaurant until late at night. During that time, Kyung-min had to endure and live with his younger brother, who was stronger and smarter than him. Sometimes he went out while waiting for his mother and got lost, but fortunately, he was able to return home with the help of the police. His exhausted mother, who worked late into the night, didn't check Kyung-min's presence, thinking he would be sleeping in his room. His clever brother, who had received the mission from his mother to take care of his brother, hid this fact to avoid being scolded. Meanwhile, Kyung-min became interested in the outside world.

But now, he comes to school every day, speaks about his thoughts, and has become a poet who writes a poem a day with beautiful words.

Hail Kyung-min, the poet!

26. My Dream Is an Information Processing Engineer

I have been responsible for a special education class within the regular school for six years now. The students placed in the special education class have educable mental disabilities, with IQ ranging from 70 to 85, placing them at the borderline level. While they are capable of receiving education in regular classes, their lower intelligence, coupled with academic and behavioral challenges, leads to a strong sense of inferiority and isolation. Moreover, due to significant intra-individual differences, their basic reading and mathematical abilities are notably inferior. However, their talents in areas such as music, art, physical education, and memorization often surpass those of typical children, creating an imbalance in their abilities. Therefore, pushing them too hard without considering their relatively lower developmental ceiling has proven to result in failure.

The significance of educating these students lies in maximizing their inherent potential, fostering their personality, and enhancing their possibilities and capabilities for social adaptation and independence.

As a special education teacher, it is my duty to believe in their inherent potential and provide appropriate educational measures and assistance to nurture them into confident individuals capable of coexisting with others, leading fulfilling lives. I have dedicated my efforts to guiding them in adapting to daily life, developing individual potentials, and uncovering hidden talents, believing that this path contributes to their vocational and social independence.

In today's advanced countries, there is an increasing awareness of the importance of special education, emphasizing an educational engineering approach. Specifically, multimedia utilization for mentally challenged children is considered effective, providing concrete situations and various auditory supports to stimulate the students' motivation and interest. Concerns about the potential failure of mentally challenged children to learn on their own, leading to frustration and a lack of recognition from parents or peers, can be alleviated through individualized learning, fostering a sense of achievement. In our classroom, thanks to the support of the school principal, we have introduced a multimedia system, including a Pentium 586, a large color monitor (37 inches), a document camera, and a color printer. With these additions, our classroom, equipped even with a karaoke machine, has become a state-of-the-art space that everyone dreams of in the 21st century.

The educational office requested the public sharing of class management practices for special education teachers. In response, I shared not only the class lessons but also the overall experiences in managing special classes, despite the emotional burden. I accepted the request with the expectation that other special classes would also adopt this system.

On the day of the demonstration research presentation, the audience included the superintendent of education, directors of the secondary education department, special education supervisors, and special education teachers from both the eastern and western regions. The event drew a large audience, enough to remove a glass window along the corridor for better viewing.

The learning theme was "Creating a Schedule Using

Word Processing Software." Using CD-ROM titles and a document camera, I focused the students' attention and reminded them of the prerequisite skills. After presenting the learning objectives and introducing the topics to be studied using the software, we proceeded to hands-on practice. The demonstration included repetitive exercises to familiarize the students with computer document processing functions, such as writing a diary and creating invitations. On this particular day, the task was to create a schedule. All 20 students operated computers, inserted floppy disks, and produced edited documents, printing them using the color printer.

After finishing the task, turning off the computers, removing the disks, and organizing them in individual disk boxes, the subsequent process of tidying up the surroundings and the teacher providing individual guidance to the students, including helping those struggling, was also observed. There were variations in speed, accuracy, and editing skills based on individual differences, but no student remained passive.

Among them, Kyung-wook's proficiency in using Word stood out. Kim has residual effects of cerebral palsy, resulting in limited finger dexterity and difficulty controlling his head movements. The observers watched the process of Kim creating his schedule on a large monitor. When he demonstrated rapid keyboard skills, accurate typing, precise mouse movements, and artistic schedule formatting with various colors, all the observers applauded in encouragement, expressing a sense of victory for humanity.

After the public class, a presentation and discussion meeting were held. Director K of the education office, during his remarks on his impressions, revealed that he couldn't stay until the end of the class. When he witnessed Kim creating his schedule, tears welled up in his eyes, and he went outside alone to cry in a corner. He mentioned that his daughter is also a child with mental development delay. 'If someone shows interest in such children, they can do it,' he said, sharing his feelings. The atmosphere inside the room became solemn. Director K promised to include the budget for the installation of multimedia systems in all special classes under the jurisdiction of the education office in the supplementary budget, a moment that brought me to tears as well.

The actual experience confirmed that the use of multimedia in teaching children with mental retardation is indeed effective, as suggested by previous research findings. In particular, using computer word processing programs for writing instruction has been very helpful for children with disabilities. Children who were once teased by their peers and siblings due to their uneven handwriting can now freely choose beautiful fonts and various colors to create documents, enabling them to grow into proactive and confident individuals.

As a result, today, I can proudly distribute personal anthologies and class anthologies, including the collection from the demonstration class. Not only that, but the path to Kyung-wook's dream of becoming an information processing specialist has opened up. He has been accepted into the business automation department of a vocational high school, securing his future.

To the future information processing specialist, dreamer, fighting!

27. Teacher's Day

It's Teacher's Day. The pathways on both sides of the school gate were bustling with flower vendors and male students eagerly waiting to buy flowers.

Whether in the city or the countryside, the flowers that middle school boys bring on Teacher's Day usually amount to nothing more than a 50 cent carnation bouquet. Some even bring fresh flowers alongside the carnation. Though it may seem formal, if the heartfelt intention of giving a single flower to a teacher is cherished throughout life, how joyful would that act be? With genuine respect and the spirit of courtesy toward the teacher, it would be a crowning achievement. Undoubtedly, it is the shared responsibility of teachers, parents, and society to nurture individuals of such distinction.

The passion of Teacher's Day lasted all day. Whether excelling in studies or not, being a model student or a troublemaker, each student meticulously divided their hard-earned allowance to buy carnations for their homeroom teacher and other subject teachers they liked. The hallways and even the teachers' offices were abuzz with activity. Each teacher's desk, stacked high with red and pink carnations, transformed the office into a floral haven. At every class period, promises were made, and fireworks exploded in various classrooms, followed immediately by singing the Teacher's Day song. A new tradition that resonates among us.

However, there were some who remained unfazed by this atmosphere, and they were none other than the students in our class. Rather than being indifferent, it would be more accurate to say they were unaware. Despite being the same age and physique as their peers, they had developmental delays, either congenital or acquired. Upon entering the classroom, instead of presenting flowers, they enthusiastically jumped around on the mats, not sparing a glance at me, their homeroom teacher.

It was time to leave. As I was walking halfway across the pedestrian crosswalk, I heard someone shout, 'Hey!

Our teacher's here!' Three young ladies rushed toward me, enveloping me in hugs and bouncing up and down. During my three years at S High School, I had been the homeroom teacher for these developmentally delayed students, who, thanks to my guidance, had transitioned to a vocational high school. Overjoyed to see them, I forgot I was in the middle of the pedestrian crosswalk and joined them in their lively sprint. One of the students had difficulty walking due to the sequelae of viral meningitis. After a brief moment, I supported her, and we returned to our path in a daze.

Once we safely crossed the road, cars sped by. Sweat dripped down my back.

The three young ladies came to visit me on Teacher's Day, adorned with roses decorated with baby's breath or gypsophila flowers. Graduating from high school and securing employment at the same electronics company, their words struck a chord, and my eyes welled with tears. Their bright, towering figures, coupled with the harmonious blend of color and design in their attire, moved me even more.

These students were just like our current students three years ago on Teacher's Day. Without the help of a teacher, they couldn't even dress themselves. Though it took a while, they continued to grow endlessly, and today, they were able to present flowers to me in such a dignified manner.

I wonder if students without disabilities, who were eagerly giving flowers to homeroom teachers and subject teachers today, will visit their old teachers after graduation, like my students with disabilities.

28. We All became Recitation Champions

Yong-min received first place in the district competition and went on to win the gold medal at the city-sponsored poetry recitation contest. He participated as the school representative because he had won a gold medal in the district competition.

During the district competition, Yong-min unexpectedly received high scores. He recited one prescribed poem and one free-form poem according to the competition rules, and even now, recalling that sight fills me with hope.

 Initially, Yong-min recited George Hoon's "Seungmu." Whether it was the accompanying background music, 'Night of the Temple,' which enhanced the atmosphere, or his ability to express the poetic mood with a combination of high and low voices, he almost perfectly delivered

the poem, showing impressive expressions and recitation skills. Next, for the free-form poem, Sowol Kim's "Cho-hon" was also expressed remarkably. Choosing a long poem, though somewhat challenging, was intentional, as it was Yong-min's specialty, and it was believed that he could achieve a high score in recitation.

On that day, when the decision for the gold medal was reached, the opinions of the judges were divided. Most teachers, including the Korean language teacher, suggested giving Yong-min a special award and awarding the gold medal to the runner-up who was in a regular class. They argued that giving a gold medal to a special education class student among 1,500 students and sending them to the city-sponsored contest was not appropriate.

Encouraged by the overwhelming support of the majority of teachers who believed it should be based on skills, I called for an emergency teachers' meeting. Yong-min was asked to recite a poem again in front of all the teachers, and finally, he was recognized as a worthy recipient of the "gold medal."

Yong-min joined our class in the second semester of his first year. He spent the whole day with his mouth tightly shut, never uttering a word. He had no friends to socialize with. His life was filled with the hardships of his father's business failure, impoverished living conditions, family discord, and, eventually, his parents' divorce, leading to separation from his mother. It must have been an ordeal for a young boy to endure.

Yet, he never rushed, nor did he force himself to speak. On days when he came to school without washing, I wiped his face, let him wash up, and even cut his hair.

In the winter, I added carrots and kimchi to cold rice, stir-fried them together, and occasionally cooked ramen and made tteokbokki. We played O-mok together on the mat, rolled around, and sang loudly in the karaoke room. During that time, we became close, and our eyes often met. His mouth finally opened around the end of the first year. His speech was unclear, making it hard to understand. However, he started reading aloud and telling stories, thanks to my encouragement. Eventually, we created a "personalized program" suitable for his abilities.

After setting up a large mirror that could reflect his whole body, we sat side by side, comparing each other's lip shapes while practicing pronunciation. Fortunately, he did not have congenital language disorders. Through reading picture books every day, telling and listening to stories, reading and writing together, we developed a bond during our time together.

When his pronunciation became clearer, I recorded his voice on a cassette tape. I analyzed the tone, pitch, and volume, while encouraging him. He seemed very satisfied. While non-disabled students received supplementary lessons for high school entrance exams, we used that time to memorize and repeatedly recite poems for a year and 10 months, aiming for the school poetry recitation contest that was going to be held in our third year.

We attended "Poetry Recitation Contests" sponsored by the Gwangju City Love Society, the Gwangju Civil Servant Association, and literary clubs, listening to recordings and repeating the process. Looking back, it is not that not be surprising that Yong-min won the gold medal at the city-sponsored poetry recitation contest.

The saying "Practice leads to success" was certainly not an empty phrase. The saying "Practice leads to success" was certainly not an empty phrase. Regardless of the challenges a child may face, they possess at least one skill. With a helping hand, there is not a single child who remains stagnant. I experienced this firsthand.

Following Yong-min, the next year, Gi-sub Ahn won the gold medal in the city-sponsored contest, and the following year, Kyung-wook Kim and Cheol-seong Kim won encouragement awards in the district competition. The wonderful tradition continued. Without any special training, they became poetry recitation champions. It was the result of imitative education.

The following year, Inju Seong won the gold medal at the city-sponsored contest, and from the second-grade class, Seok Jeong won the gold medal in the district competition and the bronze medal at the city-sponsored contest. The good tradition continued. Under the influence of imitation education, the title of "Poetry Recitation Class" was firmly established.

I presented special education case studies at the Gwangju Special Education Workshop, the Principal and Teacher Training Workshop for Special Classes in Elementary and Middle Schools, and more. All the prize-winning students proudly demonstrated their recitation skills, bringing tears to the eyes of special education officials and teachers alike. As a result, these students gained confidence. Inspired by this enjoyment, I continued to stay and work at this school, consistently producing poetry recitation champions. The future was bright.

I've chosen this job because I genuinely like it. Step by step, I will match my pace to the slow steps of the children towards new possibilities.

29. Art Festival and Poetry Exhibition

Today is the day of our school's art festival, featuring both performances and an art exhibition. The performance program showcased various categories such as choir, vocal solo, English songs, flute duet, violin solo, piano ensemble, pansori (Korean traditional storytelling through singing), traditional play, aerobics recitation, and more. The exhibition included artworks from both students and faculty members, spanning Korean painting, Western painting, posters, calligraphy, poetry, origami, ceramics, paper folding, and science box assembly. The students' attitude towards viewing the exhibits was very serious. There was no need to tell them to 'be quiet,' unlike during regular class hours. They viewed the artworks with smiles on their faces, sometimes sparkling with joy, and at other times immersed in deep contemplation. The quote from the philosopher Plato, "Art is the only means that can educate humans without using a whip," resonated deeply within me.

Amidst the intense competition for survival within the college entrance exam-oriented education system, the school, which has long been heavily focused on knowledge, has belatedly introduced a festival ground, melting frozen hearts. It is indeed fortunate to establish a festival ground where the honed skills can be shown with enthusiasm.

Our special education students could not be left out. It was a good opportunity for them to showcase the skills they had honed. All students in our class participated by submitting works in categories such as origami, ceramics, science box assembly, and poetry.

Particularly, their poetry works received praise for their excellence. They selected poems from the anthology they had created, drew suitable illustrations, and then wrote the poems in beautiful handwriting. When framed and displayed in the exhibition hall, the works stood out. Below each piece, they included a photo of the artist along with an explanation of the work.

The Regional Education Superintendent, Mr. S, spent

a considerate amount of time in front of our class students' artworks, stroking each student's head and boosting their morale. Non-disabled students also attached roses to the artworks of our class students.

While these works may not compete with those of bright and literary peers, I believe they provided confidence to students with disabilities, hope to their parents, and an opportunity for non-disabled students to break down prejudices against people with disabilities. Moreover, I am confident that it served as a catalyst for all individuals to propel themselves into action and recharge their own lives.

30. Shall I Make You a Cup of Coffee?

It was a Saturday afternoon when I visited the E Welfare Center with my fellow teacher J.

As 2 p.m. struck, the waiting room of the welfare center bustled with activity, filled with students eager to participate in the weekend leisure program for individuals with intellectual disabilities, along with volunteer assistants.

As soon as I stepped into the waiting room, a young man rushed toward me and warmly embraced me. With a loud voice, he said, "Hello, Ms. Kim. It's In-seok. Shall I make you a cup of coffee?" Without waiting for my response, he headed straight to the vending machine in the corner. This was In-seok.

To a surprised J, I briefly explained that he had graduated from C Middle School ten years ago and had been in my special education class. Although he could barely write his name and home phone number at the time of graduation, he had maintained his social and behavioral habits from the time of admission. I mentioned that he was now actively participating in the social adaptation training program offered by the welfare center.

In-seok's actions continued to astonish us. He adeptly handled the vending machine, brought two cups of coffee with flair, took cautious steps to avoid spills, and guided us to a table in the waiting room, ensuring a comfortable space for us to enjoy our coffee.

The gratitude for those who had supported In-seok over the years welled up in my eyes. J, too, seemed deeply moved. In-seok's actions kept us entertained. Suddenly dropping the bag he had been carrying all along, he pulled out a thick album, saying, "Teacher, is this the graduation gift you gave me?" and opened the first page to reveal a photo. It was a picture of me holding In-seok, dressed in a bright orange hanbok with a bouquet, on his graduation day.

This photo, taken by his sister during his high school graduation, captured a moment in time. Uncertain of when we might meet again, he had carried this photo in his bag for ten years to share it with me. The graduation gift, rather than a simple album, was a portfolio of his growth over three years of middle school. Starting with a self-introduction that he had typed out with information about his height, weight, hobbies, dreams, role models, favorite sports, athletes, singers, talents, and foods, it was a colorful print out. The rest mainly consisted of photos I had taken, depicting class photos, classroom scenes, extracurricular activities, group games with the Youth Welfare Group, field trips, sports days, outings, poetry competitions, and science projects.

There were also originals of his personal writings and artworks, certificates, and recent photos documenting his progress. It seemed that In-seok had meticulously compiled his life record, and even ten years later, he continued to carry it with him.

Reflecting on In-seok's incredible transformation, I felt a sense of shame. His mother had worked hard in a restaurant to make ends meet after losing her husband in a late-night hit-and-run accident. In-seok had taken on the responsibility of caring for his younger siblings, struggling to get by. He faced challenges in his school commute due to the bus stop's distance and his mother's work hours.

After graduating from middle school, I had recommended that In-seok enroll in the special high school department for individuals with disabilities. However, his mother strongly opposed it, citing difficulties with transportation and his safety in commuting from the bus stop to their home.

One day, not long after his graduation, In-seok's sister called me in distress. She shared that In-seok, left alone at home, often got into trouble. On that particular day, their house had been burglarized. When she scolded him for letting anyone into the house and warned him not to do it again, he became upset and accidentally shattered a large mirror by hitting it with his hand. She pleaded with me to visit and persuade their mother.

I instructed In-seok to participate in a rehabilitation program at the welfare center run by volunteers. Three years later, I changed schools and moved closer to their home. Occasionally, I would inquire about In-seok's well-being during phone calls with his sister. After that, the news abruptly stopped. His mother changed jobs, and his sister also started working in another city, making it challenging to maintain contact.

About ten years had passed, and In-seok, now twenty-five, had had transformed into a remarkably sociable young man. Although it took a long time, his mother's patient waiting and consistent participation in the social adaptation training program at the welfare center had played a crucial role in his remarkable development.

In-seok was now part of a guided tour program for individuals with intellectual disabilities, showcasing his ability to independently use public transportation, adhere to schedules, and interact well with friends. The volunteer enthusiastically praised his achievements, emphasizing his punctuality, social skills, and ability to interact with peers.

Witnessing In-seok's extraordinary journey, I felt a sense of shame. At a time when no one paid attention to the welfare policies for individuals with intellectual disabilities, the welfare center, led by Father C, initiated welfare programs early on. They laid the foundation for challenging projects like "group homes," aiming at improving the quality of life for individuals with disabilities. It was heartwarming to see such initiatives.

In line with national policies, lifelong education is actively taking place in various institutions, including universities. However, almost all of these efforts are considerations for non-disabled individuals.

Dreaming of the day when lifelong education from the rehabilitation program spreads, enhancing the quality of life for people with disabilities, I set out from the welfare center with Teacher J.

31. Ms. Kim, Did I Pass?

Today, the results of the referral-required high school entrance exam were announced. Eager to find out whether our classmate Min had been accepted, I picked up the telephone. With a pounding heart, I called out the exam number. Min, who had already noticed, approached me and, with slow but precise pronunciation, asked, "Ms. Kim, did I pass?"

I gestured by pressing my index fingers on my lips, signaling him to calm down, and quickly understood. His appearance today seemed unusually humble. At the age of only about three months, he became deaf due to the aftereffects of a fever, and on top of that, he developed a language disorder. It was challenging for such a young person to endure the pain of being a person with multiple disabilities.

Min's primary doctor opposed wearing a hearing aid, stating that there was a possibility of hearing recovery if he made an effort to listen to his parents. According to him, Min passed the entrance exam for S High School's mechanical engineering department, just as he wished.

I confirmed it once again and then exclaimed loudly, "Min, you passed! Congratulations!" I raised my thumbs and made the sign for "the best." Min hugged me, crying loudly in joy.

At the age of eighteen this year, Min is strong and energetic. His strength comes from resembling his grandfather, who, in his youth, achieved fame by wrestling and winning two bulls as a prize during wrestling matches held on Dano and Chuseok holidays.

With a black, thick beard and broad shoulders, Min is quite a young man. Whenever he cleaned, he effortlessly lifted the heavy iron cabinet and moved it around. Whenever I jokingly said, "When our Min graduates, who will move this heavy cabinet for us?" he would respond, "Just call me during the big cleaning day, I'll come and help." I would tease him like that, and he would playfully agree.

Min caused quite a stir from the day he entered school. I couldn't leave my seat even for a moment because, in my absence, he would hit other students. I would even

170

take the students to the public bus stop, ensure Min got on the bus first, confirm its departure, and only then help the other students get on other buses.

His repair skills were excellent, but acquiring language skills was a challenge, and it wasn't until the summer vacation of the third year of middle school that he managed it with difficulty. With a strong sense of pride, whenever a friend solved a problem before him, he would often leave the classroom.

Once, there was an incident. A newly graduated special education teacher was teaching math, and for some reason, Min was unhappy. He suddenly lifted his desk, hit a friend next to him, and grabbed the textbooks and notes stored in his locker, throwing them all outside. Then, he fled outside the school gate.

When I tried to chase him, he shouted, "I have 80,000 won; I'm going to Seoul. The math teacher and my dad hate me. They hate me." He ran away so fast I couldn't catch up with him. All I could do was yell back, "Our Min is smart, and he'll definitely come back. If he runs away, he might get caught by gangsters and become a pickpocket. Do you know that?" I shouted, futilely.

However, it was in vain. The despair at that moment

was unimaginable. Such an incident happened so suddenly that I couldn't seek help from those around me. The math teacher praised a friend for studying while solving a problem, and Min suddenly behaved like that. Given his history of running away during elementary school, I was even more anxious.

I reported this to Min's parents, and then I learned that Min had hit his younger brother during breakfast. His father scolded him severely, and that's when I understood the reason for his behavior. If there had been a close bond between the children and the family, this could have been prevented.

Feeling sorry for not being able to comfort the children's painful hearts, I ran to the train station, while Min's father checked the bus terminal. Just in case Min returned to school, I asked the basketball players practicing on the playground to inform me if they saw a child wandering around the school. However, Min didn't appear anywhere.

About ten minutes after filing the missing person report around 6 p.m., the basketball players ran over and said that one of the outdoor toilets was locked tightly, and it seemed like someone was inside. I had a hunch that Min was hiding inside. I knocked on the door and called out, "Min, if you're done, come out. We need to go home. I've been waiting for you to come back; our Min is loyal, indeed."

Min smiled and stuck his head out; I hugged him, patted his back, and consoled him. Since that day, Min became closer to me, even sharing details about the conflicts between his dad and mom.

Min had a talent for handcrafts; he could skillfully replicate whatever he saw. His abilities in paper folding, ceramic crafts, and assembling science boxes were excellent. With such talents, he gained confidence in achieving social independence. Having already experienced success during middle school, he was self-assured.

Although he decided to pursue a career in the mechanical engineering department of an industrial high school, literacy posed a challenge. Aware from experience that rushing or being overly ambitious leads to failure, he set a relaxed period to acquire literacy until the first semester of the third year of middle school.

Utilizing his interests and aptitude, Min aimed to participate in the science box assembly competition, practicing 30 minutes every day. There were times when he couldn't endure for more than 10 minutes and became impatient. Each time, I patiently waited for him, and he gradually started to focus on science box assembly. Sometimes, while immersing himself in the assembly, he complained that time was too short, expressing somewhat mature complaints about social life. However, at times, he would even persuade to continue practicing until 6 p.m. in the evening.

Finally, around the beginning of the third year of middle school, he managed to read textbooks bit by bit. Many positive things happened, leading to his participation in the school's science box assembly competition. He competed confidently with regular students and received an encouragement award. During the award ceremony, the principal praised Min's unwavering determination as an example for all students to follow, making Min a popular star.

Min's dream is to establish a science institute next to our school gate, and he had already decided on the name "Hyangminsa." He explained that he took the "Hyang" character from my name and added it to his name, Min.

"When you become the president, it would be great to put your name in front and call it 'Minhyangsa,'" I suggested. Min certainly disagreed, saying he would go with 'Hyangminsa.' I look forward to that awaited day.

32. Please Tell Us Hope

Today, I once again took my class students on a mountain trail. My class primarily consists of students with dual disabilities due to autism, all diagnosed with overweight or obesity, requiring regular exercise.

"Why on earth did that lady end up having four sons like that? Tsk tsk tsk..." said a lady coming down the mountain looking at me. Most people tend to evaluate others based on certain standards and judge them accordingly. Individuals that are evaluated and fall short of the set criteria, are often considered abnormal or devalued. For example, people who are financially poorer, physically weaker, overweight or underweight, or intellectually behind than others often find it difficult to live as equal members of society.

The goal of special education is to equip children with developmental delays to live as equal members of society, leading fulfilling life. Therefore, skills for self-reliance are taught, along with interpersonal skills.

Special education teachers assist individual student, guiding them hand in hand to the bathroom to teach toilet usage and the observation of bowel movements. They also accompany students to public baths, providing instruction on simple tasks such as handling fees, open closets, dressing, locking and unlocking doors, and taking a bath.

Students also learn how to use hair salons and beauty parlors, as well as how to use banks, post offices, city buses, intercity buses, trains, post offices, and banks, along with etiquette and public manners.

To integrate each student into society, their abilities need to be improved and their image needs to be enhanced in a way accepted by society. However, there are limits to improving the abilities and enhancing the image of children with developmental delays. It is impossible without a conscious reform in mindset for people to view individuals who may be financially poor, physically weak, overweight, or intellectually behind as equal members of society, regardless of their appearance or intelligence.

Above all, there needs to be a change in the awareness

of parents with children with developmental delays. The mindset that fosters pride in having a successful child but prompts shame and the concealment of a less successful child needs to change. Teachers should teach practical skills at home by practicing what they teach. For boys, fathers should hold their hands and take them to public baths and barbershops. For girls, mothers should take them to public baths and beauty parlors, teach them how to use them, and help them acquire the skills to shop at department stores or markets.

There's a saying, "Even a dog from one's home looks pretty in the south." Humans, who are superior to all things, should be no exception. First, we need to accept the presence of these children. We should not exclude them from family outings, visits to relatives, or alumni gatherings. Parents must change their consciousness to accept their children as they are, not trying to fit them into society's predefined standards.

There is a father among parents who is successfully raising a child with developmental delays. His son has a first-degree developmental delay with autistic tendencies. From appearance to intelligence, his son does not meet society's criteria. However, the father's expression is always bright, like a sunflower. It's not something that happens in a day or two. After the son finishes his schoolwork, the father spends the remaining time taking him around, teaching him social skills. This includes collecting fees when visiting trading companies, going to public baths or barber shops, taking care of complaint documents at government offices, visiting relatives and friends, going to movie theaters, department stores, large discount stores, temples, tourist attractions, and even wholesalers. The father surpasses someone who majored in special education.

During a school talent show, when his son sang in the choir, the father held a bouquet of flowers and watched with his friend, smiling happily.

Instead of expressing pity like the lady I met on the mountain path, please share words of hope. Please recognize them as they are and share their aspirations: to be respected as human beings and receive equal treatment from others. When the perception of ordinary people changes, they gain confidence that they can live confidently like everyone else.

During my special education work experience, I felt the importance of musical therapists.

33. Singing on the Stage

Today is the day of our school's talent show. It was an event specially organized to allow students with intellectual disabilities to freely unfold their dreams. The high school choir was scheduled to perform seventh in the lineup. The members, consisting of fourteen students, were mostly those with autism, who rarely engaged in communication or interaction with others.

Among them, Shin-cheol from our class was a bit more challenging. He had a tendency to be more intense, and he was unable to sit in one place for more than five minutes. Moreover, he lacked any experience of standing on a stage, adding to the concerns. Just having him stand on the stage with other kids, holding hands, and swaying his body until the choir finished would be considered a success.

Finally, it was the choir's turn. As the curtain opened,

the members appeared amidst the sparkling stage lights. They appeared sophisticated and stylish with their blue jeans, white T-shirts, white socks, white indoor shoes, and their red-hued hats. The red hat was borrowed from the high school alumni office late last night—a decision that turned out to be a good one.

Teachers and parents watching the choir were applauding with satisfaction. Children—who usually lived confined to their inner worlds and were isolated due to their lack of communication—were now standing on the stage as choir members. The joy of this achievement was beyond words.

Despite the positive atmosphere, I was anxious that Shin-cheol might run off the stage. Students held hands, swaying their arms back and forth and singing like baby birds with their mouths open for food. The first song, "Origami," ended smoothly, followed by the second song, "Dew." When they started singing the last song, "Heavenly Fairy Tale," Shin-cheol's expression began to change.

"Shin-cheol, please endure a little longer. I'm begging you," I silently pleaded, managing to catch his eyes. Perhaps sensing the plea in my eyes, he stayed on the stage until the end of the song. Not only did he stand there, but he also sang with a proud smile, even participating in the final greetings with other kids.

The audience erupted into thunderous applause from the stands. How could this happen? It was a heartwarming moment, melting away all the anxiety built up over time.

The choir performance turned out even better than expected. Despite skepticism and concerns from those around, everyone agreed it was a success.

Having high expectations for students with developmental delays may be excessive, but we must reconsider any tendency to underestimate their capabilities or to ridicule their efforts. Children with intellectual disabilities often receive subtle criticism and reprimands for awkward behavior or small mistakes, leading them to lose enthusiasm for action and undervalue their abilities. Today's stage experience could be a turning point for Shin-cheol and other students with intellectual disabilities, giving them the confidence to say, "I can do it."

I first met Shin-cheol on March 2nd. My first impression was very positive. He had a robust physique, was handsome, and looked good in gray pants paired with a matching top. During cleaning time, he diligently swept and wiped every corner of the classroom and study room.

The next day, work time began, and barely five minutes had passed when Shin-cheol suddenly stood up, went to the sink, and turned on the water faucet, letting it run excessively while washing his hands for about ten minutes. After watching him for a while, I approached him calling his name. He responded with a grunt, making rebellious noises. After a struggle, he was finally settled in his seat. However, while individually guiding other students, screams were heard. Startled, I turned around to see Shin-cheol choking a male student sitting next to him. After separating them, Shin-cheol rushed to a female student, repeating the same behavior. When I tried to stop him, this time he grabbed my head with both hands and did not let go. Fortunately, a male teacher happened to pass by and saw what was happening, so he hurried over to intervene. During the scuffle, Shin-cheol scratched the teacher's hand, resulting in injuries. When the teacher struggled to subdue him, Shin-cheol began to scream and struck his own cheek, exhibiting self-injurious behavior. He continued to bounce around the room until the floor showed signs of wear, and then, abruptly, he collapsed.

This behavior repeated the next day and the day after.

Lacking the ability to control emotions and suffering from severe language disorders, Shin-cheol was a student who did not comply with instructions easily. Violent and destructive behavior are often more prevalent in children with intellectual disabilities, especially those with autism. However, if such behavior is not corrected and is left unattended, it can lead to not only personal character disorders but also antisocial behavior, causing harm to classmates and disrupting communal life. Shin-cheol was an example of this.

Observing Shin-cheol's behavior, I felt the need to prevent the unhappiness of individual children and alleviate their anger and rage. Thus, I designed a program to facilitate a smooth social life. Yet, none of the methods such as timeouts, physically restraining him after violent outbursts, and allowing him to lie down to find emotional stability, proved effective in the long run.

Considering Shin-cheol's preference for music, I decided to try music therapy. Music therapy involves systematically using musical activities to enhance physical and mental functions, improving an individual's quality of life, and bringing about positive behavioral changes.

To gather theoretical evidence, I visited the website of S University Music Therapy Graduate School, where professional music therapists are trained. There, I found some positive and compelling information.

According to the Korean Music Therapy Society, music therapy is defined as "the systematic use of musical activities to enhance the physical and mental functions of a person, raising the quality of life and bringing about positive behavioral changes." Clinical experiences have shown that music is more effective than sedatives in reducing patient anxiety and creating a relaxed state of mind. Patients using music therapy have significantly lower stress hormone levels, including cortisol, adrenal cortical hormone, prolactin, and beta-endorphins, compared to those who do not use music therapy. This indicates that music can be used as a therapeutic agent to modify emotions.

Moreover, music therapy allows the therapy recipient to have meaningful musical experiences using the tool of music to change their behavior. These experiences include spontaneous playing of expressive improvisational music, experiences of recreating music, creative experiences of modifying song lyrics and singing them, and experiences of appreciating music.

Encouraged by this theoretical foundation, I planned to incorporate music therapy into Shin-cheol's treatment, taking into account his functional level and condition. I arranged quiet spaces both at school and at home, allowing him to spend about 30 minutes daily listening to music. When selecting songs, I first identified his musical preferences, directly asking him about the music he enjoyed listening to. I prepared a variety of music meditation videos, CDs, and tapes that included enjoyable and amusing songs to help him manage anger and find emotional stability. After observing Shin-cheol's reactions, I selected songs that were calming and played them when he showed signs of emotional distress.

Shin-cheol's favorite songs include nursery rhymes like "Folding Paper," "Dew," and "Heavenly Fairy Tale," as well as instrumental pieces like Taek-sang Nam's "Sunset by the River," "Dancing Piano," and foreign songs like "Heart," "Pianist under the Starry Night," "Rainy Afternoon," "Night and Dream," "Flower," "Two Women," "Child Playing the Piano," "Days Like a Rainbow," and "Whispers of Autumn."

Musical therapy proved to be effective. Initially unable to endure for more than 10 minutes, Shin-cheol gradually started listening for about 20 minutes during break and lunchtime, nodding his head, laughing, and even showing a sad expression while deeply immersing himself in the music.

It was evident that music held a special significance for Shin-cheol. With newfound confidence, I quickly played his favorite music whenever there were signs of unusual behavior or expressions.

Once, to test his ability to differentiate songs, I changed the tape while he briefly left his seat. He quickly noticed the change and found the correct song to continue his enjoyment.

Nowadays, he independently selects and enjoys pieces of music. If he gets tired of listening, he takes out the tape himself, even at home. The same goes for school, demonstrating his ability to manage his time without external assistance.

While logical proof is necessary for treatment results, there was a clear positive change in his behavior. The frequency of violent outbursts gradually decreased to the point where there were no incidents for three months. Moreover, he confidently stood on stage, holding hands with friends and singing. Music therapy clearly moved his emotions, providing mental stability and enhancing social functioning. Of course, the familiarity with the chosen nursery rhymes for the choir, such as "Folding Paper," "Dew," and "Heavenly Fairy Tale," played a role in motivating him and encouraging his active participation. This was made possible by the camaraderie formed between the teacher and the child.

Therefore, his musical therapy had been a highly positive experience, and plans were underway to incorporate various musical experiences such as spontaneous playing, group instrument activities, and vocal activities, alongside the musical therapy sessions.

Through this experience, I have come to realize the importance of professional music therapists.

34. Becoming a Tailor

It was during the working hours when Jun-hee used scissors to cut the straps of the just finished mat. It happened in an instant, and everyone was left dumbfounded. The atmosphere was tense. Throughout the hot summer, the students had shed sweat like beads, clumsily assembling piece by piece for a collaborative artwork intended for the school art exhibition. However, disappointment filled the air. Resentment was directed at Jun-hee, and the classroom atmosphere turned grim. I made efforts to soothe the anger of the children, convincing them that Jun-hee hadn't done it intentionally. I told that we should forgive a friend who made a mistake while finishing the work. I suggested that we consider the previous work as practice and strive to create an even better piece. The children accepted my proposal.

The next day, Jun-hee came to school with a strange hairstyle. The children laughed, but I didn't find it amusing. Surely, Jun-hee's mother must have trimmed his hair in a haphazard manner.

Jun-hee had a habit of cutting visible things with scissors almost every day—hair, clothes, friends' handicrafts, and more. The story about Jun-hee's tendency to cut hair, clothes, and friends' handicrafts with scissors was known to me from the previous homeroom teacher. However, since the new semester started and three months had passed without such incidents, I had been relieved.

I began to observe Jun-hee's maladaptive behavior more closely, considering it a problematic action. There were also instances of devouring a large amount of food at snack or mealtime and quickly getting up from the seat afterward. Jun-hee enjoyed singing along to the songs of the younger generation and dancing to the disco rhythm, displaying decent dance skills. Jun-hee liked turning the computer on and off and enjoyed embroidery.

Based on the life records and consultations with previous homeroom teachers during his elementary and middle school career, I knew that Jun-hee's habit of cutting hair, clothes, friends' handicrafts, etc., had been a problem. However, since three months into the new semester, there had been no such incidents, and I was at ease.

Next, I heard the story about Jun-hee's childhood background through counseling with parents. The family lived a middle-class life with one younger brother, and the love for Jun-hee was special. The only difference with the younger brother was that Jun-hee's language development was delayed, and from an early age, Jun-hee played alone without making eye contact with others.

To find out more specific behavioral characteristics, I conducted a diagnosis and assessment. Using standardized assessment tools, I found that the indices for language development, behavioral adaptation, play, group adaptability, and interpersonal relationships were very low, while the antisocial behavior index was high. Additionally, Jun-hee was aggressive, had a significantly low level of activity, but showed self-reliance in personal hygiene.

In cases like Jun-hee's, where applying drug therapy techniques dominated the prevailing theory for relief, I hesitated due to resistance to medication and concerns about side effects. I decided to explore alternative methods.

Based on the information gathered, I ventured into

occupational therapy. I believed that Jun-hee could experience a sense of accomplishment by assigning tasks that align with his interests and abilities, particularly in occupational skills (crafts). As a result, I focused on providing him with tasks related to his hobbies and skills.

Having confidence that if inappropriate behavior is ignored, and positive behavior is acknowledged through verbal praise and encouragement via physical contact when engaging in desirable actions, there would be an increase in positive behavior. This belief motivated my decision.

I reached out to Dr. C, a pediatric psychiatrist, and Drs. H and L, authorities in behavior modification, via email to seek advice on the information about Jun-hee and my corrective program. Trusting in their profound interest and love for children with disabilities, whom I respect more than anyone, I believed they would respond favorably. They responded with a much more compassionate and constructive reply than expected in a shorter time.

Occupational therapy, initially carried out for therapeutic reasons in hospitals and rehabilitation centers, is now widely applied. In the United States, occupational therapists are placed in schools. This therapy focuses on the physical, psychological, and communicative development of students or patients, determining their physical and mental abilities, adaptability in society, interests, work habits, and hidden occupational adaptation abilities through pre-occupational evaluation.

Feeling empowered, I began the occupational therapy program for Jun-hee, envisioning a happy future for him. Considering Jun-hee's interests and talents, I chose embroidery as the task, gradually increasing the complexity from simple designs he could handle to more diverse and intricate ones. During the activities, I created an atmosphere by playing contemporary music, such as Finkl, Diva, Onion, and H.O.T, which Jun-hee enjoyed and could sing along with.

In response to maladaptive behaviors during tasks, I provided language praise, such as "Jun-hee, you are really good at this," when he exhibited desirable behavior. Physical contact, like hugging and patting on the back, was also employed. Once the artwork was completed, it was displayed on the "Proud Corner." Though the quality of the work was lower than his peers, I attached a photo capturing the process with explanations highlighting the positive aspects.

To utilize leisure and lunchtime effectively, I organized disco time, encouraging friends and teachers to dance together. Group sound activities provided an opportunity for a long-term showcase. During sports events and talent shows, Jun-hee was cast in the lead role for the play "Chunhyangjeon" and played the role of a swallow in "Heungbujeon," showcasing his dancing skills. After the play, he was given the role of collecting props.

When not displaying problematic behaviors, Jun-hee was given reinforcement in the form of a weekly opportunity to play computer games—a pre-agreed commitment that I granted.

Jun-hee and I spent eleven months crying and sometimes laughing together. Assigning tasks that he could handle with his abilities, and sincerely performing them, Jun-hee experienced a sense of accomplishment and joy, leading to a decrease in the frequency of maladaptive behaviors.

I encouraged parents to compliment the displayed artwork on the bulletin board when they visited the school. The persistent cooperative system among experts, parents, and teachers, utilizing EduNet, yielded positive results.

Jun-hee's meticulously crafted embroidery won a gold medal at the school art exhibition, and many pieces were sold at the school bazaar. During the 'Special School Talent Show,' his excellent dancing contributed significantly to our school drama club winning an award.

These days, Jun-hee is busy showing off his portfolio: it is filled with photos of his working process and interesting descriptions.

Upon contemplation, I realized that Jun-hee was gradually forgetting the behavior of cutting and tearing with scissors because he knew that when he engaged in positive behavior, his mother, brother, relatives, and teachers recognized, praised, and caressed him. No matter how excellent the theory may be, it cannot surpass the loving care of a field teacher. Even if Jun-hee were to exhibit such behavior again, I would nurture him with the belief that "it can be done," not as an evaluating teacher but as a mother praying for the happiness of his or her children.

35. The Very Great Present

Hello, Fox Grandma! I read the Aesop's fable "The Fox and the Grapes" and decided to write you this letter. I am Ki-wook, a 16-year-old 3rd-year middle school student in Gwangju 00 School. What is your name, Fox Grandma? I'm curious about your age. My hobby is writing, and I'm wondering what your special talent is. My favorite food is pancakes. How about you, Fox Grandma? What is your favorite food?

Let me introduce my family. We have Dad, Mom, my older sister, and me - a family of four. How about your family, Fox Grandma?

I enjoy watching talents like Choi Jin-sil and Chae Si-ra, and I also like Lee Seung-yeon. Who is your favorite?

I heard you had trouble picking grapes and got upset.

Next time, if you can't reach them, try using a ladder. I'll lend you mine. Goodbye for now.

- Ki-wook, September 28, 2000

This text is a letter written by Ki-wook, a third-year middle school student, after reading "The Fox and the Grapes" from "Aesop's Fables."

I don't know if the fox is a mister or a lady. However, Ki-wook, who is currently in the third year of middle school, possesses a cunning intellect, demonstrated by his ability to calculate the degree of consanguinity after reading "Aesop's Fables" just once. Grandmother, mister, aunt, brother, sister, younger sibling, etc., various titles appear in each story, and it is surprising how well they fit the impression of each character. He calls the ants younger siblings, the doves older sisters, and the goats grandmothers.

Moreover, he goes up and down the mountain. On the day he unintentionally stepped on an ant, he apologized, saying, "Dear ant baby, I'm really sorry," and immediately wrote a letter to the ant when he returned to the classroom. Perhaps, God gave Ki-wook a clear and pure heart, along with discerning eyes, to prepare him as a writer.

Ki-wook is a boy with a mental disability at level 3 and exhibits autism tendencies, but he had outstanding characteristics. One of them is a habit that changed recently. He became fascinated by reading fairy tales and is busy writing book reports. When he writes a letter, he always uses appropriate titles like mister, lady, grandmother, sister, brother, etc., to the protagonist. The content is also clever. He encourages and advises through letters or sometimes expresses it in poetry.

Ki-wook finally submitted the carefully written book reports he collected in June to the "1st Open Literary Contest for Disabled Youth," and unexpectedly, his poem "Prince" was selected as the winning work. He became the lucky recipient of a prize of one million won, and this experience opened the door for him to become a writer.

The award ceremony was held at the National Assembly Members' Office Building, which was attended by about 300 people wishing congratulations, including the Minister of Culture, Health and Welfare, and the President of the Korean Writers' Association. It was a meaningful event that received attention, support, and applause from various fields for enhancing the cultural rights of people with disabilities and providing them with a path to participate as professional artists.

Ki-wook received a promise of continuous support for publishing works and literary debuts. He also won a gold prize in the school's book report writing contest and was selected as the "1st Reading Education Award" and "Shining Faces in Gwangju Education" by the Gwangju Metropolitan Office of Education.

Ki-wook, who had occasionally written personal collections of book reports, poems, and diaries, published a personal anthology, and he is preparing for his second volume.

Now, Ki-wook is too busy, and I, who will soon leave the teaching profession, need to give him a truly memorable gift. Even if I leave the education field, I promise to be by Ki-wook's side until he stands as a writer. The following is the poem "Prince" written by Ki-wook.

I fell asleep while reading a fairy tale book.
I shook the sleeping princess to wake her up,
And we ran away into the forest.

We fell over the tree roots

And cried out loud.

Why cry like a child?

My mom laughed and teased me.

Yes, even though he sacrificed his destiny because he is a "mentally challenged" person, what is different from other boys is his dream of becoming a prince. He is a sixteen years old boy who wants to hold the hand of a princess and live happily in an empty forest with no one else around. He holds a beautiful dream and keeps this beautiful dream in his heart.

The awards ceremony was held grandly with about 300 people, including the Minister of Culture, Health and Welfare, and the President of the Korean Literary Association, at the National Assembly Members' Building. The event, which raised awareness of cultural rights for people with disabilities, not only improved the quality of life by enhancing the cultural fragrance but also opened the way for them to participate as professional artists. It received attention, support, and applause from various fields.

Ki-wook has promised continuous support for publishing works and entering the literary world. He also won a gold prize at the school's book review writing contest and was selected for the "1st Reading Education Award" and "Faces Brightening Gwangju Education" by the Gwangju Education Office.

He has published a personal collection of book reviews, diaries, and is preparing for the second edition. Now Ki-wook is too busy to wander around the principal's office, teacher's office, or the administrative office as before. He is too engrossed in reading.

All these results are Ki-wook's pride and the pride of the special education school. It became an opportunity to instill hope and confidence to all disabled youth. It also became an opportunity to give pride to parents and teachers.

This is not something that can happen in a day or two, and it is impossible to rely on one person's strength alone. It is the result of sweat and tears made by a family, school, and society with interest and cooperation.

I firmly believe that such a day will come and I will wait for it. "If there is intelligence, there is a way to the summit."

36. Finding Pairs of Rubber Gloves

I visited a rubber glove manufacturing company in N City with my students' parents. The reason was that students who would graduate from high school in February next year were already on-site, receiving on-the-job training. The kids, who usually couldn't sit still for a moment, were actively picking out pairs of gloves from the piles with a blink of an eye, matching the right and left gloves. Among them, one child was handling the rather challenging task of accurately counting and packaging ten pairs.

Vocational education at special schools should focus on transition education centered on adult life. Transition education, part of the 7th curriculum, is a vocational curriculum tailored to the demands and characteristics of disabled youth, aiming to facilitate their transition from school to society, including further education, employment, independent living, or social participation.

Vocational education aims to help students recognize and perform their roles for living confidently as members of the local community. It acts as a bridge to move towards the local community, fostering the enthusiasm and confidence to identify and perform one's role for living. To prepare for social life, basic skills required for daily living and the foundational skills for future occupations must be acquired. Additionally, efforts should be made to connect education in schools with the post-employment process, enhancing the effectiveness of vocational rehabilitation.

With this philosophy and goal in mind, fellow teachers who share a special passion for activating vocational education—and in collaboration with "Association for Vocational Rehabilitation Curriculum for Students with Intellectual Disabilities"—have organized and established the 'Association for Vocational Rehabilitation Curriculum for Students with Intellectual Disabilities.'

We decided to operate the timetable flexibly according to the needs. This flexibility was deemed necessary to visit the field regularly to arrange employment opportunities with local companies.

We have actively promoted our close relationship with companies, which not only provides necessary support through follow-up guidance to the graduates currently employed but also contributes to the increase in the production capacity of these companies. Through this close relationship, we were able to obtain information about the required workforce and, as a result, students scheduled to graduate were able to engage in on-site training in advance.

As a preparatory process before participating in on-site training, the students first learned the local bus routes. This included understanding the travel time from home to the destination, knowing the bus numbers available, preparing and storing bus tickets or fares, learning about traffic lights, bus stops, and ticket booths, memorizing the phone number of the prospective workplace, and making a phone call.

Initially, parents would accompany them to the bus stop, but now they can independently arrive at the designated location on time. Similarly, during the return journey, the company provides transportation to the same location where the bus departed in the morning. Of course, they are punctual in their attendance. They have good interpersonal skills, receive praise from seniors, colleagues, and friends, and have learned appropriate greetings, handshakes, etc., through role-playing.

One student with limited movement in one arm was the only one excluded; however, we are confident that, with his cleverness, he will find a job that he can handle despite the slight inconvenience. According to the supervisor, Geum-hee, in our class, is quick-witted and has not made a single mistake so far.

While it was somewhat joyful to hear that everyone, except one student, was employed, it was also heartrending. Every year, graduates are produced, but due to the lack of employment opportunities, they are unable to find jobs. To achieve their goal of social independence, we must develop basic skills necessary for social life and provide them with training in foundational functions related to their future occupations. After all, isn't the purpose of education for people with disabilities social independence?

Every one of us, including myself, has some form of disability, whether big or small. The only difference is that ours might not be visible to the naked eye. However, by harboring a sense of superiority over disabled individuals, with negative and misguided stereotypes like, 'What can they accomplish?' we might inadvertently sow seeds of relative exclusion and inferiority rather than instilling hope.

If we all show interest in our marginalized neighbors, we can create a world where we can live well together. Life is positive, and disabled individuals are valuable and precious beings given by God. Regardless of their slightly unclear speech or slightly diminished cognitive abilities, they are, without a doubt, valuable and precious treasures given by God.

It is our collective responsibility to develop the residual abilities of individuals with mental and physical disabilities and provide employment opportunities suitable for their abilities. Let us all take the lead in developing the capabilities of those who desire to work with disabilities, promoting employment for disabled individuals. If we all care about our marginalized neighbors, we can create a world where we can live well together.

The mothers were looking at their sons and daughters, who were pouring their hearts into finding pairs of rubber gloves, with a sense of admiration. Tears welled up in their eyes, as if filled with emotions.

I decided to convey the feelings of the sons and daughters to their mothers.

Mother, I remember. When I was young,

Whenever you looked at me and said,

"What will become of my poor child?" with tears in your eyes.

Mother, please don't cry now.

When I get my first salary, I'll start saving, you know.

Every day, I work on finding pairs for the rubber gloves.

It laughs happily when I quickly pick out the right and left gloves from the piles like a mountain, and It cries sadly when I can't find a match.

You may not believe it, but I hear it in my ears.

Mother, please don't cry now.

Just like finding pairs of rubber gloves, I'll find my match and get married.

37. Swimmer and Volunteer

The 21st National Disabled Sports Competition, held under the slogan "Together, Strong, Until the End," took place at Busan Gudeok Stadium from May 9 to 11, 2001. The event saw the participation of 1,500 athletes competing across 17 events, including swimming.

This competition holds significant meaning for people with disabilities, serving to encourage the recovery of physical functions and boost enthusiasm for rehabilitation through sports activities. It also aims to dispel prejudices against disabled individuals within the broader non-disabled community.

Ki-wook participated as a swimmer in the 50-meter freestyle event, giving his best effort to reach the finish line. Although he did not win a medal, considering the time when he struggled to discern the direction while swimming, it was a remarkable success.

The first day Ki-wook and I went to the swimming pool was the day we had the first weekly swimming lesson. After explaining the rules of using the swimming pool, we preparing the necessary items and headed to the pool. We agreed to meet at the pool, and I sent Ki-wook to the men's changing room. However, just as I was about to enter the women's changing room, Ki-wook rushed out completely naked, his face flushed. Trying to avoid the warm glances around, I quickly pushed Ki-wook's back to the men's changing room. The men inside, who were undressing, all screamed, "Ma'am, this is the men's changing room!"

At that moment, I keenly felt the need for male volunteers.

Every time I see Ki-wook, calling male volunteers "hyung" (older brother), the awkward memory of that incident comes back, making my face turn red.

Training a developmentally delayed child as a swimmer is no easy task. Continuous guidance is only possible when the teacher discovers the potential and parents provide dedicated support. In Ki-wook's case, it was possible due to the sincere efforts of parents, the high school coach who personally engaged with local officials to connect with competent swimming instructors, and the trust, administrative, and financial support from the school.

After participating in this competition, Ki-wook seems to have grown both physically and mentally. With continuous guidance, I hope he can participate in the next competition as well.

38. Reading Guidance and Publication

It was a sunny early spring afternoon. The editorial team, along with fellow staff members, is working on editing the third edition of our school's educational materials.

As I review the manuscripts, I see a world depicted with clear eyes, a world whispered like an angel's story. There are rainbow-colored dreams of various kinds, and some writings gesturing for the warm spring sunlight to keep coming through the windows. Unknowingly, I become immersed in the world painted by the angels, the stories that feel like whispers, and the joy of walking on a rainbow-colored dream path.

The spring sunlight, which seemed to have waited and tired, crossed over the mountains, abandoning us.

This year marks the third edition of our school's educational materials. The cover of the materials, titled "I Can Do It Too," depicts brightly colored devices, and the cover features children riding in colorful vehicles, reaching towards a brilliant rainbow. It beautifully captures the image of children with developmental delays striving towards a radiant rainbow.

The content mainly consists of prize-winning works from the in-school reading expression contests held during the first and second semesters, including reading comprehension, drawings, comics, and poems created by students after reading fairy tales. Some are collaborative works by the class, while others are individual pieces. Additionally, the materials include teachers' reflections on reading, special guidance cases for students, parents' reading reflections, and child-rearing experiences.

Therefore, our school's educational materials can be considered a collection of works by students and parents. The diverse genres and heartfelt stories of child-rearing by warm-hearted individuals alleviate the shared pain of those going through similar experiences.

Among the notable works are the reading expressions, where students who cannot read independently listen to the content of a storybook from parents or teachers and then express their feelings through drawings. Reading expressions provide a message of hope not only to students with developmental delays and their parents but also to special education practitioners.

Publishing educational materials in a special needs school for students with intellectual disabilities is a challenging task. With the active support of the school principal, who enthusiastically promoted the initiative, we are now publishing the third edition. The content has become richer compared to the inaugural issue, and the reading expressions are now in color, bringing a fresh and new experience.

In 1999, the city's education office designated the popularization of reading as a special policy. Accordingly, schools at all levels formulated creative reading education plans suitable for their circumstances and actively implemented them.

However, in special education schools where the majority of students cannot acquire literacy skills, reading education was a challenging task. Nevertheless, the school staff, led by the principal, gathered with the intention of saying, "We can do it too," and even parents joined the effort.

The integrated effort of the school staff and parents led to the establishment of a creative instructional plan tailored to the imaginative world of students with intellectual disabilities, focusing on the popularization of "reading as a way of life." Activities such as teacher-parent joint reading, life-oriented reading expression through drawing, and activation of teacher-parent book clubs were implemented.

Class teachers formulated class-specific reading guidance plans based on the school's reading guidance plan, considering the individual abilities of class members. The distinctive feature of our school's reading guidance method is the focus on short, varied methods to avoid losing interest during the short time allotted, taking into account that most students cannot read.

The selection of books is based on students' abilities, including illustrated fables, scripts, songs, fairy tales, comics, and other interesting content. The teaching methods are not uniform but allow for the exercise of individual creativity within each class. Reading guidance for students with intellectual disabilities proved effective by reading books to students and eliciting answers through questions, discussing their thoughts on landscapes, people, and colors by looking at pictures together.

For example, questions like, "What color is the dress

the princess is wearing? What is your favorite color? If you were the lover of the princess or prince, what color clothes would you gift?" were used to draw out their thoughts. Furthermore, methods such as role-playing and reading aloud with teachers, exchanging roles, recording voices, and more were used to maintain interest.

As students progressed, we guided them in writing and reading expressions. Instead of rigid and formulaic reading reflections, we encouraged free and versatile expressions such as drawings, letters, and comic writing, resulting in diverse and interesting works.

To showcase the skills that the students obtained, we organized a semiannual in-school reading expression contest. One in the first semester and one in the second semester, with all students creating their works at the same time on the contest day. In the first semester, we focused mainly on collaborative class works. While in the second semester, we emphasized individual works, diversifying the content with reading expressions, comics, and reading reflections. Prizes and awards, including certificates and gift vouchers, were given to all participants, fostering a voluntary reading atmosphere.

Teachers read fairy tales to students, and eventually,

students who could compose poems emerged one by one.

Thus, the reading guidance education, which began with joint teacher-parent book reading and writing reading reflections, has settled down, making the educational materials more enriching.

Our students will continue to read books diligently, think deeply, and express the results in beautiful drawings, delightful comics, or kind words even when they become adults. My participation in this endeavor is a blessing bestowed by the divine and will be remembered as the most precious event throughout my life.

The success of the reading guidance program in a special needs school is evaluated not only for alleviating parents' prejudices against their children but also for reshaping the perception of the general public toward individuals with developmental delays and special education schools.

39. Class Journal "Blue-Colored Dream"

Children who learned to read and write Korean later than their peers, slowly navigating crooked letters, have now developed the ability to express their thoughts in writing. A remarkable achievement is that, utilizing the computer word processing program they painstakingly learned, each one typed and edited their own works to publish a class journal called "Blue-Colored Dream."

I want to share this class journal with the parents who love these children, with the teachers, and with everyone in this world who has experienced intellectual disabilities. I hope that, through the publication of the journal, I can inspire every disabled person to have confidence and think, "we can do it too."

Let's all live with confidence,
Even if we're less skilled than our younger siblings,
Because we can do it too.

Let's all live dreaming our blue dreams,
Even if we're slower than our friends or siblings,
Someday, we'll achieve those dreams.

- Author's Introduction to the First Issue of "Blue-
  Colored Dream"

The children are diligently tapping
away at the keyboard, knowing that
their carefully crafted works will
be featured in the class journal. On a
day like today, these scenes are particularly admirable.
Cheol-gyun's dedication is especially remarkable. Despite facing weak eyesight due to congenital glaucoma, he places his eyes close to the keyboard and types with determination. His actions exude a sense of confidence rather than helplessness.

Most of the students, including Cheol-gyun, fall within the borderline range, with an IQ between 70 and 85. They are children who could receive education in regular classes but also need special education. Due to their delayed learning progress compared to their peers, they lost interest in learning from elementary school. Although these children require special guidance, it's an impossible task in a mainstream class. Consequently, the gap with their peers widened.

Considering their relatively low developmental ceiling, I didn't rush things. I planned to gradually elevate their abilities. To achieve this, I had the children write a diary every day. They used known or learned words to write a titled diary, even though diaries usually don't have titles. This was a method to write diaries with key points.

I also conducted topic-based writing exercises. After selecting the topic, each child decided on their own subtopic. To show them what a topic and a subtopic are, I provided exemplary diaries and trained them to imitate.

Initially, I had them write only one story. It was to ensure that even if it wasn't an important event, the writing clearly revealed the topic. Once they reached a stage where they could write clear stories with distinct topics, I allowed them to write several stories under a unified theme.

Starting from writing three sentences under the same topic, we gradually increased to five sentences, seven sentences, and so on. It was very effective. Some of these works were included in the class journal, "Blue-Colored Dream."

Before introducing the works featured in "Blue-Colored Dream," I provided brief introductions about the students who wrote them.

Cheol-gyun, despite facing weak eyesight due to congenital glaucoma, approaches life with passion. In particular, he has an excellent sense of humor and wit, perceiving society well. When introducing himself, he confidently states that his hobbies are playing sports, his special skill is writing, his favorite song is Hyun-chul Jang's "To Walk to the Sky," and his future aspiration is to become a masseur. His parents love him dearly. Possessing the physique and basic abilities to potentially become a wrestling athlete, his parents explored ways to nurture his aptitude. Eventually, he confirmed his enrollment in a high school specializing in wrestling.

Original Book I Stepped on an Ant's Foot
by Hyang-Ja Kim

Special Needs: There May be Students With Delay But None that are Stagnant in Growth

2024. 2. 28. 1st edition publish

Author   Hyang-Ja Kim.
Translation and Illustration   Claire Cho.
Publisher   Uk-Sang Chin.
BAEKSAN Publishing Co., Ltd.

370 Hoedong-ro, Paju City, Gyeonggi Province, Republic of Korea
TEL   +82.2.914.1621.
FAX   +82.31.955.9911.
E-mail   edit@ibaeksan.kr
Homepage   www.ibaeksan.kr

ISBN   979-11-6567-787-9 03180
Price   12,000won